4/6

John Tombs

A PICTURESQUE

PROMENADE

ROUND

DORKING,

In Surrey.

——— locos lætos, et amœna vireta
Fortunatorum nemorum, sedesque beatas.——*Virgil.*

Fillbrook, *page* 176.

LONDON:
JOHN WARREN, OLD BOND-STREET.
1822.

Printed by J. and C. Adlard,
Bartholomew Close.

PREFACE.

The substance of the following pages was written amidst the delightful scenes which they attempt to delineate.

It has, however, been thought proper to incorporate their *first impressions* with subject-matter of a more extended character, in order to render the present volume acceptable to the general reader; and, with a view to this object, no diligence has been spared in collecting information from those sources, whose authenticity has already placed them high in public estimation.

The leading feature of this work, will, notwithstanding, be found in the *originality* of its DESCRIPTIVE SKETCHES. HISTORY and BIOGRAPHY, which, in all ages, have been allowed to be the most useful and interesting branches of human knowledge, have not been overlooked; but have been specially introduced, wherever they might serve to illustrate the antiquity of the country. The SKETCHES OF LIVING CHARACTERS have been gleaned with equal fidelity, from well-authenticated facts; with a due regard to the conduct by which their subjects have distinguished themselves as *public men:* and, in these sketches, the author has not suffered his candour and impartiality to be compromised by any political or party bias.

Such, in truth, are the subdivisions of the following pages: and, the author flatters himself the accuracy of his information will be considered, in adjudging their general merits. As PICTURESQUE sketches, they may not possess the vivid imagery and sublime feeling of many writers on similar subjects. To the tourist and the man of letters, the author, however, hopes his volume will prove an amusing and agreeable companion; by contributing to relieve the *ennui* of a long journey, and in adding to the general stock of topographical research: and, these being the author's primary motives, he does not hesitate in relying on the liberality of the public in judging how far he has accomplished his purpose.

The author has, further, to present his acknowledgments to the public, for the gratifying patronage which they have already conferred on his efforts; and, in conclusion, he hopes their confidence has not been misplaced.

LONDON, MARCH 30, 1822.

CONTENTS.

	Page
LETHERHEAD:	3
Thorncroft—Elm Bank	ib.
Vale House—Gibbon's Grove	4
NORBURY PARK:	ib.
The River Mole	ib.
William Lock, esq.—his fine taste	5
———— painted room	6
———————— affability to Visitors—Extent of the Estate	8
E. F. Maitland, esq.	9
Prospect from the Hills	ib.
The *ferme orné*	10
Mickleham—Its gentility	ib.
———— Sir George Talbot	11
Juniper Hill—Sir Lucas Pepys—The Bishopps	ib.
Mickleham Downs—Prospect Tower	12
Juniper Hall—Thomas Broadwood, esq.	ib.
Fredley Farm—Richard Sharpe, esq.—Box-Hill	13
Brockham Hill—M. Browne, esq.	ib.
The Holmesdale—Town of Dorking	ib.
General Reflections	14
Full-grown beech-woods	15
Description of the grounds	16
Poetical Tributes	17
———— Counsellor Hardinge—Mr. Gilpin	18
CAMILLA LACY:	ib.
General d'Arblay	ib.
Benevolent occupations—Letherhead Fair	19
Madame d'Arblay	ib.
———— her *Camilla*	20
———— her society—Character of her novels	21

CONTENTS.

	Page.
Miss S. H. Burney—Improvements at Camilla Lacy—Thomas Hudson, esq.	22
TIMBERDEN COTTAGE:	ib.
Its rustic style—Gardens and pleasure-grounds	23
WESTHUMBLE COTTAGE:	ib.
Jeremiah Dyson, esq.	ib.
——————— his active benevolence	24
E. Daniells, esq.	ib.
BURFORD LODGE:	25
Mrs. Barclay—Rural elegance—Romantic walks and bridges—Mr. Eckersale	ib.
Tribute to Shenstone	26
THE GROVE:	ib.
A rich contrast	ib.
Site of the residence—Mr. Reeves—Hermitage and circuitous walks—Tablet of moral rhymes by Mrs. Knowles	27
Gothic gates and summer houses—William Skillington, esq.	28
Residence of S. W. Singer, esq.—Gothic villa	29
Road to Denbies—A promenade	30
DENBIES:	ib.
Jonathan Tyers, esq.—Vauxhall gardens—Theatrical Devices	31
Il Penseroso—A contrast	32
Sculls and pedestals—Lady's scull	33
Gentleman's scull	34
A Penitentiary	35
Extensive gardens, &c.	36
W. J. Denison, esq. M.P.	ib.
——————— his election—political integrity	37
——————— popularity—private character—benevolence	38
RAUMER COMMON:	39
Cheerful contentment—A delightful ride	ib.
Extensive prospect—St. Paul's Cathedral, &c.—Polesden—Retreat of SHERIDAN	ib.
——————— Fetcham Park — W. A. Hankey, esq.	40

CONTENTS.

	Page.
Prospect from Denbies	40
Chalk pits—Dorking lime—Mode of traffic, &c. Lime and building mania	41
The town of Dorking—Handsome villas—A reverie	43
Contentment—Crœsus and Alexander	44
A lesson to human greatness—Dwellings of the antients	45
Primeval simplicity—Savage and civilized life	46
Descent from Denbies	47
THE TOWN OF DORKING:	47
West-street Chapel—The High-street	ib.
King's Head Inn	ib.
————— its former celebrity	ib.
————— decline of	48
Theatricals, neglect of—Paving and lighting the streets	ib.
Public spirit	49
————— improvements—"London in miniature"	50
"The Library"—principle of	ib.
Book Society	51
Magazine Society	ib.
————— detailed plan of	52
Discussion Societies	54
Conversaziones	55
Etymology of "Dorking"—Salmon's conjectures	56
A radical error—Antiquity of the town	57
Customs of the manor	58
Stane-street—Popular superstition	59
Historical facts	60
THE CHURCH—Exterior of	ib.
————— conjectures exploded—St. Mary Overie	61
————— Interior of—Hatchments and tablets	62
————— Public tribute to the Earl of Rothes—Talbot family	63
————— Grand Oratorio—The chancel—A. Tucker, esq.	64
————— Jeremiah Markland—Dormitory of the Howards	65
————— Interment of the last Duke of Norfolk	ib.

	Page.
The Duke of Norfolk—His style and titles	68
——————— Political inflexibility—Talent as an agriculturist	69
——————— His rent-roll	70
——————— Eccentric habits	71
Charitable societies—Their success	72
Provident Institutions	73
——————— principles of	74
Public Schools—Bible Society and Savings Bank—Private benevolence	75
"The Press"	76
The Bank—Red Lion Inn—Gentleman's Dorking Club	77
The Red Lion ball-room	78
——————— garden—Concerts, balls, and public dinners	79
Well-regulated amusements	80
The Market-house	ib.
——————— A compromise—"The wheat-sheaf boy"	81
Dorking fowls	82
URBS IN RURE—Messrs. Burridge and Co.'s tanning establishment	83
An important discovery—Remarkable caves—A ruinous hobby	84
The Rev. John Mason's residence—His "Self-knowledge"—Biography of	85
SHRUB HILL:	87
The Earl of Rothes—Historical memoirs of	ib.
——————— His family	91
——————— death—Public character	92
Lady Rothes and the Ladies Leslie—A happy retreat	93
Slopes and shrubbery walks	94
COTMANDENE COTTAGE:	ib.
Dedric Smith, esq.—His taste and ingenuity	ib.
A cabinet collection of curiosities	95
COTMANDENE:	ib.
Salmon's account	ib.
Cottages and Alms-houses—Matches of cricket	96

CONTENTS.

	Page.
THE ENVIRONS OF DORKING:	97
Dr. Aikin—View of the town	ib.
POPULATION OF DORKING:	99
Pauperism	ib.
Parochial jurisprudence	100
ROSE HILL:	ib.
Richard Lowndes, esq.	ib.
Shrubbery and gardens	101
A meadow prospect	ib.
Guildford-road	ib.
SAND PLACE:	ib.
The Sondes	ib.
Hugh Bishopp, esq.	102
MILTON COURT:	102
Its antiquity	ib.
Jeremiah Markland	ib.
————, His retirement	103
———————— benevolence	104
———————————— death	105
Dr. Heberden	ib.
Markland's literary industry	106
Antient hospitality—The *shadow* for the substance	107
Harvest-homes and dances—Retrospection	108
Milton Manor—Antiquity of—Milton Heath	109
Historical traditions	110
BURY HILL:	111
A pleasant drive—E. Walter, esq.—Hills and plantations	ib.
"The Nower"	112
The mansion—Prospect from	113
General description of the grounds	114
Cottages and Girls' School	116
Robert Barclay, esq.	117
———————, His public and private worth	119
A benevolent circle	120
Prison discipline	ib.

CONTENTS.

	Page.
HAMLET OF MILTON:	121
A cottage scene	122
Grape-vines	123
Hogarth's "Cottage of Industry"—A sketch from humble life—Bury-Hill Gardens, &c.	124
WESTCOTT:	125
Antiquity of the manor—Site of an antient castle	ib.
Aubrey and Gough	126
Village simplicity	127
Westcott Hill—Mrs. Hibbert's *cottage-orné*	128
Interesting prospect	ib.
—————— its poetic features	130
Bloomfield and Clare	ib.
Effect of sublime scenery	131
Wotton Rectory	ib.
WOTTON CHURCH:	ib.
Monuments and tablets—Tribute to the memory of the Earl of Rothes	132
Burial-place of the Steeres—Gigantic skeleton—Dormitory of the Evelyns	133
Epitaph on John Evelyn	134
The Church-yard—Peter Campbell, esq.	136
Mr. Glanvill's bequest	137
Village funerals	138
Planting and decorating graves	ib.
————————— Evelyn's Sylva—Camden's Britannia	139
————————— Aubrey—Shakspeare—Hainanese custom	140
————————— *The Sketch Book.*	
Antiquity of Wotton	142
Oakwood Chapel	143
ABINGER:	ib.
The Church	ib.
Parkhurst—Abinger Common—A village landscape	144
Abinger Hall—James Scarlett, esq. M.P.—Road to Leith Hill	145
Wotton Park-gate	ib.
WOTTON PLACE:	ib.
Site of the residence—The Evelyns	146

	Page
John Evelyn, esq.	ib.
———————, His birth and family	148
——————————education—death of his father	149
————————— travels	150
————————— marriage	151
———————, Sayes Court—The Czar of Muscovy	152
———————, His study of gardening—Epitome of his times	153
———————, His gardens and plantations	154
———————, The Plague of London	155
———————, The Fire of London—Corruption of the court	156
———————, His retirement to Wotton—His death—His public worth	157
———————, His *Sylva* and *Memoirs*	158
———————, W. Bray, esq.	159
———————, Foundation of Greenwich Hospital—The Royal Society—A philosophical college	160
———————, His shrievalty — Horace Walpole's Catalogue of Engravers	161
———————, Retrospect of his life	162
———————, His literary contemporaries	163
Antiquity of the mansion	164
Sir John and Sir Frederick Evelyn	165
The Library	ib.
———————, Collection of books — Valuable transcripts	166
———————, Political *jeux d'esprits*—Portrait of the philosopher—The park and grounds	167
Allegorical temple, &c.—Evelyn's "*Elysium Britannicum*"	168
Lady Evelyn	ib.
———————, Her greenhouse—Her death—Her kindness to the poor	169
John Evelyn, esq.	ib.
Junction of the streams—Their former importance—Powder, brass, and fulling mills	170
The Rookery:	171
A. Tucker, esq.	ib.

CONTENTS.

	Page.
D. Malthus, esq.—Richard Fuller, esq.—The Residence	172
Description of the Grounds—Fishing House	173
———————— Rustic Temple	175
———————— View of Bury Hill	176
FILBROOK LODGE:	176
Situation of the Residence—Artificial Embellishments—curious Cascade *(see title-page)*	ib.
Fishing Hut, &c.—Shrubbery Walks, &c.	177
MAG'S WELL:	178
Meriden Farm	ib.
An interesting Excursion	179
Analysis of the Water	182
WINTERFIELD FARM:	ib.
Anglo-Saxon Coins—Extract from the *Archæologia*	183
Broadmoor	186
LEITH-HILL:	ib.
Dennis's Description	187
Mr. Bucke	189
Reflections on the Prospect	190
Visit to Leith-Hill during a Storm—Extent of the Prospect	192
Box-Hill and Norbury	193
London, Highgate and Hampstead, Harrow and Windsor	194
Leith-Hill Tower	ib.
——————, Inscriptions	195
——————, Richard Hull, esq.	ib.
——————, Ruinous State of the Walls	196
Leith-Hill Fair	198
——————, suppression of	199
Leith-Hill Place—Mr. Hull	200
TANHURST:	ib.
Sir Samuel and Lady Romilly	ib.
COLDHARBOUR:	201
Public Schools	ib.
Romantic character of the dell	202
OCKLEY:	ib.
Antiquity of the manor—Lee Steere Steere, esq.	ib.

	Page.
Elderslie Lodge—Oakley Court—Defeat of the Danes—Planting and decorating graves—Economical substitute	203
ANSTIEBURY:	204
Roman encampment	ib.
Redland and the Holmwood Hills—Frederick Arnaud Clarke, esq.—Groves and walks	205
Boar Hill	206
THE HOLMWOOD:	ib.
Cottages and Orchards—Reigate	ib.
Red deer—Strawberries—Antient farms	207
HENFOLD:	ib.
Charles Duke of Norfolk—Residence of F. A. Clarke, esq.	208
Sylvan scenery	209
BROOMHALLS:	ib.
C. W. Collins, esq.	ib.
LYNE:	ib.
J. Broadwood, esq.	ib.
BROCKHAM GREEN:	ib.
Cottage residences	210
BROCKHAM COURT LODGE	ib.
Capt. Charles Morris—His poetical talent	ib.
———————, "The old Whig poet to his old buff waistcoat"	211
———————, his convivial celebrity	212
———————, his family	213
BETCHWORTH:	ib.
Right Hon. H. Goulburn	ib.
WONHAM:	214
Viscount Templetown	ib.
BROOM:	ib.
W. Kenrick, esq.—Walks and plantations	ib.
Sawing mill—Tranquil Dale	215
BETCHWORTH CASTLE:	ib.

	Page.
The Brownes and Fenwickes—A. Tucker, esq.—Henry Peters, esq.—His shrievalty	216
Site of the Castle—Lawns, walks, &c.—Rural architecture	217
The Park—Avenues	218
———— Summer retreat	219
CHART PARK:	ib.
Sir Charles Talbot—The Vineyard	ib.
Thomas Hope, esq.—Family mausoleum	220
DORKING'S GLORY:	221
THE DEEPDENE:	222
Panoramic views—Aubrey's visit—*A long hope*	ib.
————, subterranean passage	223
Salmon's conjectures	224
Landscape gardening—Verses by Lady Burrell—The Hon. C. Howard—Laboratory and oratory	226
The Duchess of Norfolk	227
Thomas Hope, esq.—Thorvalsden—Anastasius	228
————————, Northern critics—superior taste	229
————————, his public-spirited liberality	230
The road to Reigate	231
PIPBROOK HOUSE	ib.
W. Crawford, esq.	ib.
BOX-HILL	231
Brockham-Hill—Camden	232
Erroneous assertions—Antiquity of the spot—Aubrey's description—Philip Luckombe	233
The Palace of Venus	234
Remarkable snails—Produce of the Box	235
Gilpin—Evelyn	236
THE GARDEN OF SURREY	237
Major Labelliere—*Original memoirs and anecdote of*	ib.
——————, his burial-place	238
Variegated prospects—Burford and the Grove—Westhumble	239
Letherhead and Epsom—Kingston and Esher	240
Dorking—Sussex and the South Downs—A retrospect—Love of the country	241
John Dennis	242

	Page.
Walks on the hill—The river Mole	243
Mr. Middleton on the Swallows	244
Aubrey and Salmon—Pope's *Windsor Forest*— The Hare and Hounds Inn—A dark walk	245
Nelson and Lady Hamilton	247

BURFORD BRIDGE: .... ib.
Mrs. Barbauld—"*The Cottage that stands at the foot of the Hill*" .... ib.

A BILL OF FARE: .... ib.
Concluding reflections 248

ERRATA.

Page 102, line 13, for *hither* read *here*.
—— 108, —— 17, for *healthful* read *unbroken*

A PICTURESQUE PROMENADE
ROUND
DORKING.

―――――

Like the bee sipping nectar from the choicest flowers, man may find among the works of Nature an inexhaustible theme for inquiry and discussion. The contemplative may glean from the combined beauties of woods and groves, the purling of streams, the rippling of brooks, and the fertility of hills and dales, a diversified infinity of scope for the indulgence of his natural predilections; in those successions of unsophisticated charms which baffle the inventions of art by their inimitable perfection.

On a single survey, the soul swells with inspiring awe: imaginative fancy recals to our memory the sylvans, the heroes, and the deities of the pastoral Muse, while the whole *phantasmagoria* of ideal invention becomes one busy scene of action. Sometimes we are wooing Nature amidst her renascent forms of buds and leaflets, and spangled meadows, presenting rich contrasts in their variety of colours : next comes the lovely luxuriance of Summer, to tempt us with the exquisite productions of our gardens, and undulating fields; resembling so many seas of promised plenteousness : then, the shady magnificence of Autumn, with all its golden tints and gorgeous hues, to lecture us in its scenes of falling grandeur : and last comes stern and hoary Winter, attended by his chilling attributes of frosts, and snows, and storms. Thus the vast volume of the creation is continually affording a compendium of every thing that is capable of awakening our faculties, and enabling us to be at once wise and happy. Such are the institutes of an inscrutable Omniscience, which the base ingratitude of man too often perverts by vice, infidelity, and guilt.

No period is, however, calculated to awaken more interesting sensations, than that of the commencement of day. The refrigerant mists are gradually unveiling the summits of the distant heights; the warblings of undissembled joy are reiterating throughout the landscape, and harmonizing with the ecstasy of responsive gratitude. The tinkling monotony of the sheep-bell proclaims the well-timed order of industry, and satirizes the enervating habits of indolence and sloth. The sun gilds the horizon with the refulgence of his rising beams; the turmoil of rural labour begins; and all nature appears bursting into illimitable activity.

Such was the scene I beheld on quitting the pleasant village of LETHERHEAD, on a fine sunny morning in ———. I noticed some handsome villas contiguous to the road, particularly *Thorncroft*, the seat of J. Stirling, esq.; and *Elm Bank*, the residence of W. S. Clarke, esq. adjoining which is *Vale House*, the property of T. Dickens, esq.; also *Gibbon's Grove*, the seat of H. Boulton, esq. Turning in from the road, I entered the princely domain of *Norbury Park*. I crossed the river Mole, and bent my course towards the mansion which stands on the crest of a commanding eminence, but is not easily discernible in the ascent. I frequently halted to admire the luxuriant clothing of the hills, and the beauties of the out-stretched vale, which proportionally became more striking on my approach to the summit. Box-wood, which, in all seasons, lends a main charm to this country, in this spot grows in wild profusion, and, intermingling its hues, gives a peculiar richness of effect to the whole scene. The meadow, beneath, is irregularly studded with full-grown trees, whilst its borders are watered by the meanderings of the Mole. I soon reached the mansion, which is partly surrounded by stately and wide-spreading beeches, sheltering a fine slip of lawn in the front.

Norbury Park was for some time the seat of William Lock, esq. whose father purchased it in 1764. The estate was many years possessed by the ancient family of Stydolfe, a name well known in this and the adjoining counties, ever since the Conquest; but which family declining in a female, the property came into the possession of the Tryons; from them it passed to Mr. Chapman, of whom Mr. Lock purchased the estate, with all its manorial appendages. The old mansion-house stood on the lower side of the park, near the road; but, being in a ruinous state, Mr. Lock pulled down the greater part of it, and erected the present noble mansion.

The late Mr. Lock was both a warm admirer and patron of the fine arts; particularly in the departments of sculpture and painting. On completing his mansion, he conceived an original and ingenious design of uniting the grand amphitheatre of nature, viewed from the windows of his saloon, with the masterpiece of the late *Barrett's* inimitable pencil. The magnificent scenery with which he has embellished the walls, is artfully managed to appear as a continuation of the view; introducing, in the western compartment, an assemblage of the lakes and mountains in Cumberland and Westmoreland, blended together, and forming a landscape, expressive of the most majestic idea of rural grandeur. The rude crags and distant summit of Skiddaw are contrasted with the placid meer below, which seems genially heated by the rays of a summer's setting sun, rendered more brilliant in effect by the tints of a retiring storm, shadowing the mountain's side.—The *second* compartment presents a nearer view of immense rocks, in the dreary complexion of those stupendous deserts; the sun here scarcely sheds a ray to cheer the gloomy scene.

—The fire-place forms the *third*; the chimney-glass being so let into the wall, that, were it not for the real appearance of the hearth, imagination would suggest the entrance to an elegant arbour.—In the *fourth* compartment the scene is continued, but with the placid effect of evening serenity: here the shepherd is telling his amorous tale to the attentive fair one. This scene opens to an organ, with a figure of St. Cecilia by *Cipriani*, who painted the landscape figures, as did *Gilpin* the cattle.—The ocean, bounded on one hand by hills and rocks, with a variety of characteristic accompaniments, complete the *fifth* scene.—The ceiling represents a corresponding sky, seen through a circular treillage, by *Pastorini;* and the carpet resembles a new-mown lawn. The whole is admirably connected with the view from the saloon windows, and calculated to convey a classical idea of a perfect landscape.

Mr. Lock's *painted room*, consequently,

soon became a subject of much conversation among the lovers of the picturesque; and has long been the *primum mobile* of attraction, especially as it is the only successful attempt of the kind in this country. The mansion was also enriched with several fine productions of sculpture: added to this the liberal proprietor became proverbial among his visitors, for the uniform affability of his manners, in personally conducting them through his rooms.

This estate contains 527 acres; 197 of which are occupied by parks and pleasure-grounds, 124 by the woods and plantations, 60 by arable land, and 146 by meadows, gardens, &c. The whole property, with its appurtenances, was sold by Mr. Robins, in June 1819, to F. Robinson, esq. for £19,600, without including the value of the timber; and was subsequently sold to E. F. Maitland, esq. the present proprietor. On Mr. Lock's family quitting *Norbury*, the estate remained some time unoccupied, for want of a purchaser, during which the house became out of repair, and the grounds were constantly exposed to the wantonness of many evil-disposed depredators. Mr. Maitland has re-stuccoed the front of the mansion, and enclosed the park with a new fence, which are the only improvements made since the estate has been in that gentleman's possession. A collection of several articles of household furniture, together with a few paintings and busts, belonging to the Lock family, were recently put up by auction: the respected name of Cipriani, however, attracted but few votaries; and it seems the unsuccessful sale of these *morceaux* did not much reflect on the taste and *vertu* of the inhabitants of this district.

The prospect from the *Norbury Hills* is indeed of the finest order. Majestic eminences encircle the landscape, and screen a track of country, interesting to every lover of the sublime, both from its natural beauty and artificial embellishments. To the north, a large expanse of country presents a varied and magnificent scene. Immediately at the foot of the hill is a neat *ferme orné*, the only vestige of the old mansion, now used as a farming establishment. On the right of it is Mickleham, a few years since consisting of only straggling cottages, but afterwards converted by wealthier inhabitants into a genteel village. The church, although not distinguished by its architecture, is more complete in the interior, than its exterior induces the stranger to expect. The street consists of some neat houses, chiefly occupied by families of fortune, a respectable inn, and a few smaller dwellings. Several of the villas are sheltered from the road by brick walls, which give the village a heavy and uninteresting appearance; but each of them possesses a track of pleasure-ground behind, which is laid out with much œconomy and tastefulness of design. The handsome residence, on leaving the village, is the property of Sir Geo. Talbot, bart., who added the noble colonnade.

MICKLEHAM is skirted by *Juniper-hill*, from whose healthy and flourishing plantations rises the elegant villa of Sir Lucas Pepys, bart., a gentleman of great celebrity in the medical world. In those classic shades, Sir Lucas, no doubt, passes many peaceful hours, doubly sweet to a mind well stored by philosophical research, and refined by the higher pursuits of scientific knowledge. The house was built by the late Mr. David Jenkinson, the lottery-contractor; and, in digging for the foundation, two human skeletons, a spear-head, and other exuviæ of warfare, were found. The plantations were raised by the late Sir Cecil Bishopp, bart.*

---

* The Bishopps are descended from an old Saxon family of Sussex. Many of them have sat in Parliament. The present Lord de la Zouch, in 1799, represented the borough of Bramber. In 1796 he was returned for New Shoreham, a place once famous for corruption, which circumstance produced an extension of the elective franchise. For this place he was, in 1802, returned without opposition, about

Bordering on this delightful estate, are fine open downs, on the left; and on the right is a tower, curiously built of flints, and designed, by its founder,* for an observatory, or prospect-room. This idea was probably suggested by the well-known tower on *Leith-hill*.

The valley at the foot of the downs consists of a spacious park, in which stands *Juniper-hall*, viz. the commodious mansion and offices of Thomas Broadwood, esq., the celebrated piano-forte manufacturer. The house is encompassed with cedars† of immense growth, whose deep hues give an air of sacred solemnity to the spot. The park is enclosed by a neat fence, and abounds with many charming sites for meditation and retirement. Across the paddock, opposite,

---

which time he became a claimant for the very old and dormant peerage of De-la-Zouch, which, after a long and arduous struggle, he obtained. His ancestors received the title of Baronet from James II.

* T. BROADWOOD, Esq.

† These trees are said to be of the finest growth in England. Their sombre foliage, combined with the solitary beauty of the park, may be said to bring into recollection the hallowed groves of once-famed *Lebanon*.

Juniper-hall, is *Fredley-farm*, the delightful retreat of Richard Sharpe, esq. the late member for Port-Arlington, in which station he displayed great patriotism and erudition in the popular cause.

The next object in the chain, is *Box-hill*, whose chalky steeps, chequered with its native evergreen, and thick clumps, resembling so many sequestered arbours, contribute much to the sublimity and picturesque beauty of the scene. *Box-hill* is succeeded by *Brockham-hill*, on the crest of which is the neat residence of Mackley Browne, esq. The range beyond *Brockham-hill* presents little more than a bare mountain-like appearance. The vale, or intermediate space, is filled up with the rough and woody track of *Holmesdale*, teeming with all the historic reminiscences of olden-times: successions of retired hamlets, extensive parks, fields, and well-wooded pleasure-grounds; and the town of *Dorking* and its neighbourhood, thickly studded with handsome seats and villas: the whole extending from thence to *Mickleham*, and forming a *coup-d'œil* of unparalleled richness and grandeur.

I stood musing on the fascinating scene, which successively prompted the liveliest associations of rural industry and happiness. In him who wisely appreciates the sweets of a country life, the most clinging ideas are awakened by the contemplation of so glorious a scene; and even the masterpieces of a Claude, a Poussin, or a Barrett, almost sink into insignificance, when compared with the charms of a richly-cultivated landscape. Fields, hills, villas, spiry villages, and farm-houses, crowd on the view, and create more *brilliancy of thought*, than art with all her gaudy trappings could invent. Contrast and combination succeed each other with inconceivable rapidity, and the eye lingers on the several objects, while the descriptive power of the pen is lost in their exhaustless variety;—subjects worthy of the more exalted lays of Byron, Scott, Campbell, Southey, or Moore.

Descending from the lawn through full-grown beech-woods, numerous walks intersect the dell, the eye occasionally bursting on the prospect beneath. The remains of a decayed green-house, some old rustic seats, and a few traces of trodden-down parterres, were evident marks of woful neglect, indicating that this spot had formerly been a favourite resort; and, consequently, that more pains had once been bestowed on keeping it in order. I much regretted to find so delightful a site completely neglected, and suffered to remain unnoticed. How soon, and at how trifling an expence, might a material change be effected. A pair of shears would lop off the luxuriating twigs which shoot forth and even render the access difficult. A few hours' labour would clear away the rubbish which disgraces the spot; and thus a fine site would be prepared for the erection of a tasteful edifice, to be occasionally used as a reading or prospect room. Surely the proprietor would be happier in adding to the enjoyment of well-disposed visitants than in seeing his property thus become a mere wilderness. Certain regulations and restrictions might be contrived to exclude the idle and ill-disposed from participation in such privileges; and, in cases of detection, to bring them to exemplary punishment. Is it not grievous to reflect, that, on account of the mischievous frolics of a few wanton urchins, an estate of 527 acres in extent should be denied public inspection; and that notice-boards should threaten us with frivolous prosecutions for every instance in which we might be tempted to deviate from the accustomed path? Doubtless, these measures were originally devised for the correction of malicious depredators; and not for the indiscriminate exclusion of rational visitors, who have, ever, been far from abusing public-spirited liberality, by such mean and pitiful acts.

I found the dell possessed several retired haunts, which made me still more concerned for their wild and neglected state. A small green wicket opened to a narrow walk of singular beauty, overhung by trees, which, uniting at the top, formed an arch of thick foliage. I rambled through these cool retreats, amusing myself with exploring their several windings, and enjoying the uninterrupted tranquillity of their shady nooks. The effect of such scenery on great minds is always truly imposing and impressive. In the hospitable mansion, and the delightful rides and walks of *Norbury Park*, ROYALTY has often found a happy asylum, when the factions of party-spirit and private pique inflicted irreparable inroads on conjugal and domestic comfort. Poetry has likewise availed herself of so noble a theme, and distinguished the taste and courtesy of its former proprietor in lines of uncommon felicity of expression.*

On the borders of *Norbury Park* is *Camilla Lacy*, the property of Thomas Hudson, esq. The house was built by Mr. Lock for his friend Gen. d'Arblay, who served under Louis XVI., and, subsequent to his flight from France, married Miss Burney, the authoress of Camilla, from which work this seat took its name. Here she resided for some time, upon intimate terms

---

* Sonnet to *William Lock, esq.*, written at *Norbury Park*, his beautiful country-seat.—1786.

<pre>
Favourite of Science, and in Arts refined,
That Leisure's path adorn! enraptur'd still
The living *models* view, that *Grecian* skill
Drew from that *beauty* of the *perfect Mind*,
Whose breath to Nature every form assign'd
Of captivating *grace!* The picture fill
With glowing hues—or dress the waving hill
In *Fancy's* robe; that now the touch may find
(So light the hand,) that in the fairy scene
Enamour'd stray, as by a wood-nymph led
With musing thought. But envied be the great
Exploring Goodness, by the world unseen,
Whose bounty guards from want the rustic shed,
And silent halls thee in the village bless'd.
                    Hardinge's Miscellaneous Works, vol. ii.
</pre>

Mr. Gilpin's Poem on Landscape Painting, likewise, contains the following eulogy:

<pre>
———————If taste, correct and pure,
Grounded on practice; or, what more avails
Than practice, observation justly form'd
Of Nature's best examples and effects,
Approve thy landscape; if judicious Lock
See not an error he would wish remov'd;
Then boldly deem thyself the heir of fame.
</pre>

with Mr. Lock and his family. Among the many laudable exertions of Madame d'Arblay, ought to be mentioned her co-operation with the Misses Lock in the benevolent occupation of manufacturing fancy articles, such as *card-cases, pin-cushions, work-boxes, &c.* which were annually sold at *Letherhead Fair*, and the money appropriated to charitable purposes. The Misses Lock attended personally in a booth at the fair, which was for many years well-attended by the most respectable families in the neighbourhood. Long lines of carriages might be seen there; and, on that day, the road was generally thronged with vehicles, and many hundreds of pedestrians: but, since the departure of these amiable benefactresses, this festival has much declined, both in extent and respectability.

From the family of Mr. Lock, Madame d'Arblay is supposed to have taken the models of the characters, which she has so ably displayed in the pages of *Camilla*, that masterpiece of her novels. Her morning hours were usually dedicated to the composition of the " Picture of Youth ;" which affords many instructive beacons to the tender novice, and furnishes him with those axioms, by which he may not only evade the dangers that beset him, but likewise secure the road to ease and honorable independence.

Camilla, possessing strong recommendations in its leading characters being sketched from so estimable a circle, was crowned with success, hitherto unprecedented in the annals of *novel-writing ;* and so highly did its distinguished authoress rank in public favour, that every circulating library had either her *Evelina, Cecilia,* or *Camilla;* while all these frequently possessed a place on the book-shelves of the wealthier classes. The long subscription-list prefixed to the last of these works will best prove the high repute in which Madame d'Arblay stood at that time. She continued to reside at this cottage, after the publication of *Camilla*, until she quitted England, in company with her virtuous husband, for the continent.

Madame d'Arblay has long enjoyed the best literary society of her time. Among her earlier acquaintance were Dr. Johnson, Sir Joshua Reynolds, and Edmund Burke. On several occasions she was honoured by the royal notice, by which means she became appointed to a lucrative office in the establishment. The scenes and pursuits of high life did not, however, accord with the taste or constitution of the then Miss Burney; and, grateful for the liberality and condescension of her patroness, she soon resigned her situation, and exchanged the gaiety of a court for the more pure and lasting joys of rural retirement.

As an authoress, Madame d'Arblay has taken the celebrated Richardson for her model, by making fiction a teacher of truth: in this beneficial labour she is assisted by *Augustus La Fontaine, Madame de Genlis, Miss Edgeworth, Mrs. West*, and several more of our ingenious countrywomen, who are equally entitled to patronage and esteem. In the superior talents of Miss S. H. Burney, the sister of Madame d'Arblay, the reading circles have long found an extensive fund of refined amusement, in novels of the higher order of composition, and which have proved a considerable source of emolument to our fair authoress.

Camilla Lacy has been much enlarged, and has undergone many improvements by its respective occupants. Its present proprietor has done much towards a judicious disposal of the pleasure-grounds, and the exterior embellishment and internal comforts of the villa.

Adjoining the grounds of *Camilla Lacy*, is *Timberden*, the tasteful cottage-ornée of Mrs. Bolton, eligibly placed on a knoll, and commanding picturesque views in every direction. It is built in the true rustic style, (partly *thatched*,) and was formerly an ordinary cottage; but, having been altered with much taste and expense, it forms a pleasing object in the landscape, viewed from the surrounding eminences. The front, looking towards Box Hill, is screened by a shrubbery, enclosed with neat palisades. The back is fitted up with a viranda, communicating with a small flower-garden, and, from its windows, possesses a fine view of the *Norbury Hills*.

Besides *Timberden*, *Westhumble-street* contains a neat cottage, long occupied by Jeremiah Dyson, esq. late deputy-clerk of the House of Commons. Here he occasionally retired from the fatigues of his arduous office, and enjoyed the best society in the neighbourhood. To the literary exertions of Mr. Dyson, the gentry of this part are peculiarly indebted for the formation of their book-society, which is now one of the best regulated establishments in the county, and includes in its list nearly every family of distinction in and near *Dorking*.

To the active benevolence of Mr. D. and his family, the peasantry of *Westhumble* will long bear testimony. Alternately employed in visiting their cottages, they not only afforded them temporary assistance, but, with their sympathy and consolation, inculcated many useful and important lessons. It is but justice to add, that, in these charitable acts, Mr. D. was warmly seconded by the other gentry of the hamlet, which can be traced in their unostensive methods of diffusing the first rudiments of education among the junior branches, and in the judicious circulation of moral instruction among the heads of poor families. *Westhumble Cottage* is now occupied by E. Daniells, esq. an eminent barrister of Lincoln's Inn.

Westhumble-street communicates with the high road opposite *Burford-gate*, leading, by a handsome sweep, to the neat residence of Mrs. George Barclay.* Perhaps no place can furnish a more unique picture of rural elegance, than that which this enchanting spot presents. The cottage opens on a rich carpet of verdure, while groupes of cattle feeding in its domain give it the character of a pastoral landscape. The borders are washed by the Mole, and on the bank is a neatly-trimmed path, communicating by wooden bridges with several romantic walks on Box-Hill, which, with its venerable heights, shelters the whole estate. Mr. Eckersale, to whom this property belonged in 1786, planted a part of it with choice exotics, and planned several winding walks. Here, also, he erected a votive pedestal and urn, to the memory of the poet SHENSTONE, the

---

* G. Barclay, Esq. late M.P. for Bridport, was well known as an active magistrate in this county. He died in a fit of apoplexy, in 1819, and was buried at Mickleham.

former of which bore the following appropriate inscription :

D. M. S.
Gulielmus
Shenstone
B. D. I. E.

> To the bard of Leasowe's grove,
>   Tears of silent tribute lend ;
> Scenes like these he lov'd to rove,
>   Nature's to the Muses friend.
>
> Tho' no more the path he guides,
>   Through the dell's embowering shade,
> Still his spirit there presides,
>   Still his urn shall deck the glade.

I turned down a pleasant lane on the left, in which are the respective boundaries of the Burford estate and the *Grove*. The road led me to the brink of the river, which is frequently so shallow in this part, as to admit of crossing with little difficulty. The grounds of the Grove slope by a grassy bank to the river, in which is a small waterfall ; and the neat and cultivated aspect on the one side, presents a strong contrast with the wild luxuriance at the foot of the hill, on the other.

The residence, so far from being an important structure, is a curious thatched cottage, situated in a dell, and almost entirely obscured from view, by the massy foliage of the trees, which embosom it on every side. Mr. Reeves, the original projector, spent much of his time in improving this spot. Here he formed a sequestered hermitage, and several circuitous walks, in which he contrived to introduce tablets of moral rhymes, equally happy in the sweetness of their versification, as in the tact of their general appropriation; among these are the following lines, written by Mrs. Knowles, wife of the late Dr. K. :

> Come, gentle wand'rer!—sit and rest;
>   No more the winding maze pursue;
> Art thou of solitude in quest?
>   Pause here and take the solemn view.
>
> Behold this spirit-calming vale!
>   Here stillness reigns—'tis stillness all;
> Unless is heard some warbling tale,
>   Or distant sound of waterfall.

> The letter'd stone, the Gothic gate,
>   The hermit's long forsaken cell,
> Warn thee of thy approaching fate:
>   O fear to die—not living well.
>
> But, if in virtue thou increase
>   Thou'lt bear life's ill, nor fear to die;
> Then every breeze will waft thee peace,
>   And foretaste sweet of promis'd joy.
>   M. K. 1782.

These agreeable sentimentalities were affixed to Gothic gates, and ornamental seats and summer-houses. Several of the inscriptions were copied from Denbies. The grounds communicate with the road by a green-painted lattice-gate; the whole are œconomically arranged, and abound with unceasing variety, although occupying but a small space. Notwithstanding all these attractions, the Grove has fallen into the hands of several new proprietors during a few years. It was for some time occupied by the Marquis of Wellesley; after which it came into the possession of Zadig Levin, esq. who disposed of it to the present proprietor, W. Skillington, esq. Since that period, it has occasionally been occupied by families of distinction, but merely as a summer retreat. Mr. Skillington has long contemplated the erection of a villa on a more favourable site than that of the old one; which design, if carried into execution, would greatly tend to enhance the property in public estimation, and consequently ensure it a longer tenure. Mr. Skillington resides in the small neat cottage, at the corner of the Grove.

Contiguous to this estate is the modern cottage-residence of S. W. Singer, esq. known in the literary world as the author of a curious and entertaining work, entitled "Researches into the History of Playing Cards," &c.; and as the editor of the late Mr. Spence's piquant anecdotes of Pope and his contemporaries. The front of the residence looks towards Box-Hill, and the whole forms a well-chosen retirement for a man of letters. In the spacious meadow adjoining, is a classically-elegant Gothic villa, built by Mr. Skillington, and now in the occupation of J. Savage, esq.

I returned through the lane, and directed my steps towards *Denbies*, the seat of William Joseph Denison, esq. M. P. The approach is by a fine sweep of road, recently made at the private expense of this gentleman. By taking a circuitous route, the acclivity is considerably lessened; and, besides being a valuable acquisition to the estate, this road bids fair to rival its opposite neighbour, in affording some of the finest views of the fascinating landscape, from which it gradually rises. Part of the line is already planted with trees on each side; and, from the uniform liberality of its proprietor, we may venture to expect, that, ere long, we shall be gratified in seeing it become a popular promenade. The road passes a beautiful terrace-walk, backed by a bushy wall of verdure, and leads by a noble carriage-drive to the portico of the mansion.

The house, a modern stuccoed edifice,

was built by the late Mr. Jonathan Tyers,* an ingenious and eccentric gentleman, to whom we are indebted for the establishment of Vauxhall Gardens.† At Denbies he passed much of his time in planning several theatrical allusions and devices, and in rendering this spot a perfect contrast to the bewitching routine of gaiety and merriment, with which he electrified his metropolitan votaries. The anomaly is said to have been conducted with strict adherence to that effect. Here every object tended to impress the mind with grave contemplation, and led to a conviction of the frivolity of the celebrated resort at Vauxhall, then in the zenith of its success.

---

* This residence was an obscure farm house in Mr. Tyers's time, but it has been successively altered by its respective occupiers.

† Mr. Tyers took a lease of these premises in 1730, and opened them with an advertisement of a *Ridotto al Fresco*. The novelty of this term attracted great numbers, and Mr. T.'s success induced him to open the gardens every evening during summer. They are now under the direction of Mr. Barrett, son of Bryant Barrett, Esq. who married the grand-daughter of Mr. Tyers.

The principal scene was a wood of eight acres, denominated *Il Penseroso*, where he contrived to represent, in terrific similitude, the " Valley of the Shadow of Death." Here, instead of protracted vistas of festive lamps, with their matchless reflection, and long rows of boxes containing groupes of lively gallantry, was the stillness of the mazy walk!—Instead of the choral orchestra, —a small temple, on which were numerous inscriptions, calculated to produce the most gloomy effect on their reader.—Instead of captivating glees, airs, and ballads, and the heavenly harmony of instruments,—the monotonous solo of a clock (concealed from view) broke the solemn silence at the end of every minute, and, forcibly proclaiming the rapid march of Time, served as a memento of its vast importance.— Instead of the spacious rotunda, saloons, and piazzas,—a dismal alcove, in which were some curious paintings by *Hayman*, particularly the *dying Christian* and the *unbeliever*, and a statue of *Truth* trampling on a mask, directed the attention to those awful objects.

At the termination of a walk were two elegantly-carved pedestals with two human sculls, each of which addressed the male and female visitant.

THE LADY'S SCULL.

Blush not, ye fair, to own me!—but be wise,
Nor turn from sad mortality your eyes;
Fame says (and Fame alone can tell how true)
I—once—was lovely, and belov'd—like you,
Where are my vot'ries, where my flatterers now?
Fled with the subject of each lover's vow.
Adieu the roses red, and lilies white;
Adieu those eyes, that made the darkness light.
No more, alas! those coral lips are seen,
Nor longer breathes the fragrant gale between.
Turn from your mirror, and behold in me,
At once what thousands can't or dare not see.

34 A PROMENADE

Unvarnish'd, I the real truth impart,
Nor here am plac'd, but to direct the heart.
Survey me well, ye fair ones, and believe,
The grave may terrify, but can't deceive.
On beauty's fragile state no more depend;
Here youth and pleasure, age and sorrow end.
Here drops the mask, here shuts the final scene,
Nor differs grave three-score from gay fifteen.
All press alike to the same goal—the tomb,
Where wrinkled Laura smiles at Chloe's bloom:
When coxcombs flatter, and when fools adore,
Here learn the lesson, to be vain no more.
Yet virtue still against decay can arm,
And even lend mortality a charm.

THE GENTLEMAN'S SCULL.

Why start?—the case is yours—or will be soon;
Some years, perhaps—perhaps another moon;
Life, at its utmost length, is still a breath,
And those who longest dream, must wake in death.
Like you, I once thought every bliss secure,
And gold, of ev'ry ill, the certain cure;
Till steep'd in sorrow, and besieged with pain,
Too late, I found all earthly riches vain;

Disease, with scorn, threw back the sordid fee,
And Death still answer'd, what is gold to me!
Fame, titles, honours, next I vainly sought;
And fools obsequious nurs'd the childish thought.
Circled with brib'd applause and purchas'd praise,
I built on endless grandeur, endless days;
'Till death awoke me from my dream of pride,
And laid a prouder beggar by my side.
Pleasure I courted, and obey'd my taste,
The banquet smil'd, and smil'd the gay repast;
A loathsome carcase was my constant care,
And worlds were ransack'd, but for me to share.
Go on vain man, to luxury be firm,
Yet know—I feasted but to feast a worm!
Already, sure, less terrible I seem;
And you, like me, shall own—that life's a dream.
Farewell! remember! nor my words despise—
The only happy are the only wise.

Such eccentric imageries, wrought up as irrefragable appeals to the dissolute debauchee, might form a persuasive PENITENTIARY, and urge the necessity of amendment with better effect than all the farcical frenzies of mere formalists and fanatics. They were, however, entirely removed by the Hon. Peter King, who, on the death of Mr. Tyers, in 1767, purchased the estate, which, in 1781, he disposed of to James Whyte, Esq. By the latter gentleman it was sold, in 1787, to Joseph Denison, Esq., the father of the present proprietor.

Mr. Denison has expended considerable sums in enlarging and improving the residence, and making the establishment of the completest order. The gardens, which are very extensive, are well planned, under the superintendence of a scientific and experienced horticulturist; and, indeed, the whole estate exhibits continued proofs of the superior capabilities of this gentleman, and reflects high credit on the department he so ably sustains. The house is surrounded, in front, by a pleasant lawn, interspersed with parterres of flowers, and clumps of shrubs and evergreens.

As a gentleman of the strictest honour and integrity, in his commercial negociations, Mr. Denison ranks high in the mercantile world. It was not, however, until the general election of 1818, that Mr. D. became, what may be termed, a public character. A requisition being presented to him, signed by the leading political characters, Mr. D. became a candidate for the representation of the county of Surrey in parliament, and was returned without opposition ; and, no new candidate appearing in 1820, Mr. D. and his colleague were, of course, re-elected.

In his parliamentary career, Mr. Denison has maintained a clear and consistent course, by supporting every motion to preserve the rights of the people from the encroachments of unjust power: and, although not distinguished in the ardour of debate, his name will generally be found in the lists of those inflexible and conscientious advocates for constitutional liberty, whose probity and vigilance will long shine in the records of parliamentary history. As a proof of Mr. D.'s popularity, it may be worthy of notice, that, on canvassing the county, the hundred of Wotton almost unanimously declared in his favour ; and, by the INFLEXIBILITY of his political professions, he has done high honour to the exalted station, to which his individual merits, as much as his popular public principles, so justly entitle him.

In private life, Mr. Denison is equally beloved and esteemed for the unaffected pleasantry of his general deportment. In all benevolent undertakings, he evinces that tender sympathy for the sufferings of his fellow-creatures, which forms so admirable a trait in the character of the patriot and philanthropist. In patronizing the many laudable institutions of this neighbourhood, as well as of his country at large, his zeal is unabated; and, for innumerable unostentatious acts of private munificence, his worth will long continue to be appreciated.

Adjoining Denbies is *Ranmer Common*, from the highest point of which, I discerned the dome and pinnacles of St. Paul's Cathedral and Westminster Abbey, at a distance of 25 miles; and the royal heights of Windsor, towering in the horizon of the beautiful panoramic landscape. The common is besprinkled with cottages, occupied by the labouring poor, with their well-cropped gardens and all the unpretending humility of cheerful contentment. From hence the common extends several miles, over which is a delightful ride towards Guildford, on the ridge of a range of chalk hills, commanding views of a fine scope of country on all sides.

At a short distance are the stately beech-woods of *Polesden*, formerly the retreat of the illustrious SHERIDAN, who, after captivating his admiring countrymen by the brilliancy of his wit and eloquence, occasionally retired here, and enjoyed the private society of a few select contemporaries.* Amidst the groves and walks of this sequestered spot, he passed the happy intervals of public life, awhile forgetting the angry invectives of party, in affording the world successive specimens of his prolific genius. This property is now in the possession of Richard Bonsor, esq. who has built a new residence, and has otherwise considerably improved the estate. Beyond *Polesden* are the full-grown woods of *Fetcham Park,* embosoming the fine seat of W. A. Hankey, esq., an opulent banker of the metropolis.

After wandering through the wood, which had once been the scene of Mr. Tyers's ingenuity, I returned to Denbies; and, resting myself on a rustic fence, at the extremity of the lawn, I took a complete survey of the subjacent valley.

---

* On Mr. Sheridan's marriage with the youngest daughter of the late Dr. Newton Ogle, this estate was purchased, chiefly with her fortune.
Annual Biography, 1817.

In the descent, I noticed some tremendous precipices and chalk-pits, which are continually wrought, and afford a lime much esteemed by builders, for its property of hardening under water.

This extensive establishment, which for some years past has furnished employment for a considerable number of the poor, has materially suffered by an influx of competitors, and a variety of other means, which have greatly tended to depreciate the article in the market. The *building-mania* in and near London continued to support an active, and, probably, a lucrative concern, the demands being very rapid, and the profits fully adequate to the expectations of those who embarked in the undertaking. The ordinary mode of traffic consisted in sending the lime by teams to London, and sometimes to Kingston from whence it was conveyed by barges. The teams and barges were loaded back with coals,' and thus a kind of barter was kept up between the parties. The lime-merchant, consequently, became also a coal-merchant, and a flourishing trade was carried on. This, however, was not of long duration; some of the principal consumers of the article, in the metropolis, purchased an estate in the county of Kent, capable of producing chalk, which they esteemed equal to that dug here. Added to this, the *lime-mania* infected the speculatists of Dorking as much as the *building-mania* did those of London;—a strong contest ensued—the demand soon decreased—the ordinary evils of opposition succeeded—the article fell in general estimation—and the whole concern suffered a severe shock. Notwithstanding these adverse circumstances, the traffic is still considerable, although distributed in more hands. The original establishment below Denbies is by far the most extensive, and has immense kilns, and accommodations for carrying on an important trade.

The most prominent object in the prospect from this magnificent hill is the town of DORKING, surrounded by handsome villas and genteel cottage-residences. At the back of the principal street is the parish-church, suggesting a very correct idea of the injudicious arrangement of its interior. Besides Dorking, almost all the places seen from Norbury are comprised in the view from Denbies, and which may, perhaps, be said to rival the former hills, in the beauty and variety of the scenery viewed from its summit.

While surveying the mansions of splendour and affluence which embellish the face of this country, and contrasting them with the humble cottages in the same scene, I employed myself in forming a comparative estimate as to the respective fortunes of their inmates. "*Luxury is the sweetener of life*," and, without its fortuitous aid, the incessant perplexities of the world would work on our sensibilities with redoubled effect. Contentment is alike the main prop of human happiness, and which, although it cannot be claimed as the exclusive right of wealth, must totally depend on the appropriation of the means we possess. Daily observation and experience prove to us, that the life of the man of £50,000 per annum must not be taken as a true criterion of real happiness.

Wealth is rather the glare and tinsel of luxury, than the specific means of adding to main comforts. Thus, rank and fortune impose upon their possessors the observance of certain restrictions, which reduce their lives to a mere series of ceremonious formality, to the utter exclusion of all solid enjoyment. Crœsus, the Lydian monarch, confessed the veracity of the Spartan maxim, "*that poverty was a happier state than riches*," in an expiatory ejaculation, when on the funeral pile, before the relenting Conqueror. Thus, thrones become playthings in the hands of fate, and lineage may soon be extirpated by the *fiat* of death; and, however great may be the disparity, PHILOSOPHY still defines the precept to the meanest of mankind, and adapts it to the ultimate reformation of their follies and misdeeds.

Here I saw buildings of every order; from the thatched roof, and simply-elegant villa, to the substantial brick mansion, with its contingent offices; and each of them placed in a suitable lawn, park, or court, intersected with gravelled paths or drives. I could not help remarking what contemptible huts must have been the dwellings of our forefathers, with their moveable windows, and furniture, which, in this age, a peasant would scarcely own: how miserable must have been the cottages of single rooms without stories or chimneys, and how incompetent to the methodical arrangement of a farm-house of the present day. What wretched tenements must have been the habitations of those who, in the time of Edward I. were thought rich with £30 per annum. The usual simplicity of those times will, however, account for many seeming improbabilities. In the reigns of Edward I. and Henry IV. the people possessed no foreign luxuries; employed no male servants; and even the knight, with all his chivalrous exploits, was looked upon as extremely rich with £150 per annum. The expense of college was £5; a counsellor's fee 3s. 8d., and 4d. *for his dinner!* Needle-work was also confined to ladies of superior rank until the 15th or 16th centuries. Every branch of expenditure has consequently been regulated by the refinements and superfluities which have been successively introduced into civilized life: as they have brought pleasure, they have tinctured its enjoyment with pain; and thus, amidst all our perfection, we may be almost tempted to look back on the chronicles of our ancestors, and envy them in their woods and caves, and painted skins, and the various characteristics of savage life.

I descended the hill by a steep chalky road, and, wishing to avail myself of a visit to the town of DORKING, I turned off to the left. The street, although narrow, contains several substantial dwelling-houses, built with more regard to comfort, than to mere external elegance. On the left side is a gate, leading to *West-street* chapel; and at a short distance beyond it, on the opposite side, is a small meeting-house, belonging to the Society of Friends.

This road leads into the High-street of the town, which at once bespeaks the importance and respectability of its inhabitants. At the left corner is an extensive range of building, formerly known as the *King's Head Inn*. The accommodations of this vast establishment were once on the completest scale; and, at that period, it was noted for serving up *water-sousey*, a delicate fish, in great repute among the *bon-vivants* of the town. Concerts, balls, evening parties, and convivial meetings, alternately filled its spacious and commodious rooms with crowds of company; and hence became the focus of public amusement, no less celebrated, in its time, than the most fashionable of our metropolitan resorts. This establishment, however, declined with the liberality of the age, and the premises were partly let off and converted into shops, and partly occupied by poor families. A long room was reserved by the proprietor, which was occasionally let to companies of players; and thus the spirit of mirth which once reigned within its walls, became momentarily revived. Theatricals, at length, not meeting with their due encouragement, the room was subdivided, in which state it is now occupied.

The streets of the town were well paved in the years 1817-18, before which time their imperfect state was a subject of general animadversion. The expense of paving, although of itself a formidable obstacle to the undertaking, was speedily overcome by committees of public-spirited gentlemen, to whom too much credit cannot be given for so material an embellishment to the town. The *Lighting* of the streets was the next object of concern with the individuals from whom the project of *Paving* had emanated; and, after much exertion, this addition was made in a style by no means disreputable to any city in the empire.

Some idea may be formed of the expenses of these embellishments from the amount of the bills for paving and lighting the south side of the town; the former being £317, and the latter £63, for the lamps, &c. besides the annual charge for lighting. The practicability of this scheme could only be supported by the diligence and activity of the parties; and the above line being completed, proved a strong inducement for similar exertions in the other districts of the town.

These public improvements have excited a correspondent activity among the individuals themselves. Several old houses have been pulled down, and new ones erected; others have been refronted; windows have been thrown out with increasing diligence; and Dorking may now be said to resemble "a London in miniature," possessing shops, little inferior in taste and display to the boasted lines of Cheapside or the Strand. These have proved ostensive advantages to the speculator, and, it is feared, have too frequently operated as inducements to greater undertakings than have been found to realize his expectations. A wealthy and populous neighbourhood, however, supports a trade of some consideration; while industry and integrity uniformly characterize an honourable and respectable class of tradesmen.

The intellectual habits of so worthy a community naturally awaken some interest as to their public institutions. A Circulating Library, on a scale more liberal to the public, than profitable to its proprietor, offers a series of reading, beyond the ordinary compass of so limited a collection; the enlargement of the stock being regulated rather by the improving literary merits of the age, than by a speculative spirit of enterprize on the part of the conductor, who, consequently, regards the selection of his numbers as a primary motive. A Book-society has for some time been established among the gentry of the town and neighbourhood, and which, under the same judicious superintendance as originally formed, will continue to maintain its decided superiority over many similar societies.

Literature has also found a sufficient number of votaries to establish a Magazine-society among the townsmen; and, although the only one in the place, its plan has been circulated; and generally adopted in several other towns, where simultaneous efforts have been made to add to the comforts and amusements of domestic and social life.*

---

* The formation of these societies is said to have *originated* with a bookseller, in a populous town in the north of England, who, in a short space of time, formed no less than *ten* such establishments in his own neighbourhood. The idea was warmly seconded, and extensively promulgated through the medium of a widely-circulating London Miscellany. The cause could not have fallen into more able hands. The plan suggested was simple and effectual in its operation, and, of course, soon recommended itself to the attention of several active booksellers in various parts of the kingdom. Newspaper clubs had long been censured for the pernicious habits which they encouraged, and consequently were on the wane. The ascendancy which the magazine-press had already gained in the conduct of each department, and the literary œconomy of the proposed system, acted as strong inducements to the reading-public; and in the course of a few months, nearly every town in the empire boasted of its magazine-society, while large districts frequently had six or more of these institutions, according to the extent and habits of the population.

About this time, an individual, who, from motives of delicacy is not here named, chanced to meet the editor of the journal, to whose efforts magazine-societies owe much of their popularity and recommendation. The scheme of forming a magazine-society at Dorking was suggested,

Book-knowledge, however, loses many of its fascinating attractions by too close

---

The idea was earnestly received by the individual already alluded to, and, shortly after this, he circulated a set of written proposals among the reading families of that town. He soon had the pleasure to find he had not mistaken the tenor of public opinion; for, scarcely three weeks had elapsed, before twenty individuals subscribed themselves as members, at 15s. per annum, which, with his own subscription, amounted to fifteen guineas. A fund being thus constituted for one year, he proposed the following

List of Works.—Monthly Magazine. Baldwin's London Magazine. The Eclectic Review. The Imperial Magazine. Blackwood's Edinburgh Magazine. Monthly Review. Journal of Modern Voyages and Travels.—*Reviews.* Edinburgh, Quarterly, and British. Time's Telescope.
The six first works were regularly put in circulation on the second day of the month; the Journal of Voyages and Travels on the day after publication; the Reviews every quarter, on the day after their respective deliveries in the metropolis; and Time's Telescope annually.

This list being unanimously approved, the circulation commenced on October 1, 1820. Thus, for the trifling sum of *fifteen shillings per annum*, paid in advance, each subscriber was supplied in *rotation* with *seven* of the most popular monthly journals, and three reviews quarterly; affording, collectively, a series of intellectual entertainment during the whole year: amounting in the aggregate to *one hundred* numbers, and no fewer than *one thousand hours' reading*, besides a joint property in the stock at the expiration of the year.

an intimacy, and requires frequent incentives to preserve its popularity; otherwise, reading would be thought little more than a method of filling up the surplusage of time. The literary circles of Dorking might soon obtain the desideratum which is so strikingly evident amongst them, by forming *Societies for the discussion of*

The practicability of the Dorking plan soon induced the author to publish it in the pages of the Monthly Magazine, with a view of affording publicity to a scheme, already sanctioned by general approbation.

The bookseller's bill, and a few incidentals for books, paper, and printing, amounted to fifteen guineas, the sum originally subscribed; and at the termination of the year, it was proposed to sell the magazines, &c. by auction, and transfer the produce to the subsequent year's account. Various circumstances, however, prevented the writer from witnessing the execution of that part of the plan. The general principle of the scheme will, nevertheless, long continue a favourite with the public; and afford satisfaction to those who feel interested in its success, and endeavour to promote its object by their gratuitous services.—For a set of regulations, a copy of a book list, and miscellaneous information on this subject, see the *Monthly Magazine*, vol. 50—51.

moral, political and philosophical topics, selected from the floating incidents of life, according to their relations to the public welfare :

—————————" with sense refin'd
Learning digested well—————
Unstudied wit, and humour ever gay,
 *   *   *   *
To raise the sacred hour, to bid it smile,
And with the social spirit warm the heart."
                              Thomson.

These institutions, partaking of the character of dilettanti-societies, and conversaziones, would enable their members to form more accurate estimates of the merits of general literature. At the same time, by connecting much practical information in the various branches of science, with a fund of unceasing interest, these societies would tend to cultivate and enrich the mind, and impart an additional relish for researches of a higher order.

The etymology of the name of this parish appears long to have been a subject of much dispute. Salmon, an authentic topographical writer of the last century, mentions "the common *error* of the maps, in writing it with an *a*; for, it should be Dorking, as many gentlemen of the town assert." In his "*New Survey of England*," published in 1726, he says,

"I crave no favour for writing it with an *a*, Dorking, because I am well assured it is not yet out of use, in conveyances and publick writings. There are two villages in *Essex*, near Tilbury-Fort, called *Thurrack*, and one in *Hertfordshire*, named *Thorocking*, which signifies an oak consecrated to *Thor* the *Saxon* idol, whence our *Thursday*. That our ancestors dedicated trees and groves to the worship of their gods, is plain from *Tacitus, Lib. de Morib. Germ. cap.* 9. *Gildas* also saith, they paid divine honours to mountains, rivers, fountains, groves."

"Supposing then, them that came after took the usual liberty of pronouncing *D* for *Th*, as frequently they did on the contrary *Th* for *D*, the name from *Thorocking* might easily come to *Dorocking*, and thence to *Dorking*, for further I am not concerned to carry it."

The post-office stamp has long been

"Darking;" in consequence of which, the error has been readily admitted into *Directories, Gazetteers*, and various topographical works; but, with the exception of the above instance, and a few unauthorized presumptions, the *o* is now universally adopted.

According to historical record, the town was destroyed by the incursions of the Danes, but rebuilt either by Canute or the Normans. From the domesday survey, the manor appears to have been one of those held by Edith, queen of Edward the Confessor, but then in the possession of the Conqueror. After its alienation from the crown, the earls of Warren are the first subjects in whose hands it is found. From that family, it descended to the Fitz-Alans, earls of Arundel; and on the decease of Thomas, the last earl without issue, in 1415, his estates were divided among his three sisters. On this partition, Reigate and Dorking were carried by Elizabeth, the eldest, into the family of the Mowbrays, dukes of Norfolk. The latter becoming extinct on the death of Anne, who was married to the duke of York, the second son of Edward IV., the manor of Dorking was divided among the descendants of the four daughters of the above-mentioned Elizabeth Fitz-Alan. Three of the four parts soon became united in the illustrious house of Norfolk; and the other fourth was purchased of the late Sir Henry St. John Mildmay, bart. by the late duke, who thus became possessed of the whole, after it had been divided more than three hundred years. Among the peculiar usages of this manor, it may be remarked, that the custom of borough English prevails here, by which the youngest son inherits the copyhold.

Salmon mentions, that Dorking was probably a considerable place since the Sussex road here fell in with the Ermine, and that there was no other station, either in Sussex or Surrey, at the time of Antoninus Pius. The former of these roads, the Stane-street, or Roman road, leading from Arundel to Dorking, is said to have passed through the church-yard, and to have been frequently discovered there in digging the graves. In the parish of Ockley, to the south of Dorking, this road, for the space of two miles, is used as a highway, under the name of *Stane-Street Causeway*. The *Magna Britannia*, speaking of this part of it, describes the road as formed of flints and pebbles, and says, that, because there are no materials of the kind near it, the common people ascribe the work to infernal agency.

Antiquarians have already expended much time and research in exploring the primitive history of this parish, the details of which will, of course, be found at length in the county history edited by Messrs. Manning and Bray. Sufficient authority has already been quoted to prove the antiquity of Dorking; and, from many singular coincidences of facts, names, and dates, it has, doubtless, been the field of some of those sanguinary conflicts, mentioned in the records of our earliest times. No remains of Roman buildings have, however, been discovered in the immediate vicinity, but the rude vestigia of several military stations may still be traced in the neighbourhood.

A small gate on the left side of the street opens to a broad flagged walk, leading to the church-porch. The church consists of a nave, with north and south aisles, and a chancel divided from the former by a transept, in the centre of which is a low tower, containing eight bells and a set of chimes. The whole is built of the ordinary stone and flints of the country, except the upper part of the tower, which is composed of squared stone or chalk. Various orders of building denote the additions and enlargements made by successive generations, and present a curious compound of antique and modern architecture. The tradition of the inhabitants is, that it was erected by the founder of *St. Mary Overie*, in *Southwark*. There is little, however, in the structure of Dorking church, to authenticate this assertion. St. Mary Overie, (now St. Saviour)[*] is distinguished by its unique and beautiful Gothic order; and abounds with the rich tracery of pointed windows, and many highly-interesting specimens of ecclesiastical architecture. These have already been the subjects of much studious and diligent enquiry. In the course of this investigation, nothing has transpired to warrant the above tradition; and, if we may judge from the respective buildings,

---

[*] Dugdale ascribes the foundation of this monastic pile, to Bishop Giffard (or Gifford,) about the year 1106. *Hist. and Antiq. of St. Saviour.*

no very conclusive idea can be drawn: for, while the one affords a treasury of antiquarian relics for the gratification of the curious mind,—the other is altogether destitute of these attractions, and presents an incongruous, and comparatively uninteresting, appearance.

The interior of the church is rather injudiciously planned, the pews being allotted with little uniformity or œconomy of arrangement. There are, however, a few commodious family-seats, whose matted floors and neatly-covered sides denote the superior rank of their proprietors. The walls exhibit the usual plainness of decoration of a country church, except the faded emblazonry of a few family hatchments, and two or three neat monuments to the memory of departed worth. On the right of a glazed door, leading from the middle aisle, through the transept to the chancel, is an elegant tablet, erected by public subscription, and bearing the following classically-written inscription, on a slab of white marble:

To the Memory
of the Right Honourable
George William Evelyn, Earl of Rothes, Baron Leslie and Bambreigh,
one of the sixteen Scotch Peers,
and Colonel of the Surrey Yeomanry Cavalry, from their first enrolment :
who departed out of this Life on the eleventh Day of February, MDCCCXVII.
in the forty-ninth Year of his Age.
after a constant Residence in this Town for twenty-five Years ;
during which eventful period, comprehending the whole war with revolutionary France,
His Lordship was uniformly actuated by a zeal
for the Public Good ;
and shone before Men an eminent example of Loyalty to his Sovereign,
of reverence for the Civil and Religious establishments of his Country,
of ardour in his Military Command,
and of Moderation and Equity in the Local Administration of Justice:
whilst in Private Life he conciliated the respect and love of all Classes
by the urbanity of his Deportment,
by the warmth of his Friendship, by the cheerfulness of his convivial Conversation,
and
by the exercise of every conjugal, paternal, domestic, and social Virtue :
The Inhabitants of Dorking,
deeply affected by the awful suddenness of his Dissolution,
grateful for the Benefits, which he conferred upon them,
and desirous of perpetuating their cordial sense of his transcendent Merits,
have caused
this Monument to be erected.

On the other side of the door is a tablet, to the memory of the deceased members of the Talbot family, late of Chart Park. The whole is surmounted with a neat stone pediment, corresponding with the first-mentioned monument.

Over the door is a large board, enumerating the several donations to the poor of the parish; and above this, are tablets of the commandments, &c. and whole-length paintings of Moses and Aaron in their robes of office. Several devices and allegorical representations fill up the spacious tablature, reaching to the roof, and forming a group of interesting scenic design.

In August, 1818, a grand oratorio and selection of sacred music were performed here, under the superintendance of the celebrated Mr. C. J. Ashley. The undertaking was liberally patronized by the high-sheriff, and several other gentlemen of distinction in the neighbourhood, and passed off with great eclat, affording a treat to the amateurs and lovers of sacred melody.

The chancel contains some handsome hatchments and monuments, among which is one of Abraham Tucker, esq. formerly of Betchworth Castle, who died in 1774. Here is also a small brass plate, with an inscription to the memory of the celebrated Jeremiah Markland, from the pen of his learned friend, Dr. Heberden.

The north end of the transept serves for a vestry, in which is the burial-place of the family of the HOWARDS.—The interment of Charles Howard, the eleventh and last duke of Norfolk took place here on the 23d. of December, 1815, with great pomp and solemnity. The procession left Norfolk House, St. James's Square, about nine o'clock in the morning, composed of the coach and six horses of H. R. H. the Duke of Sussex, and nearly twenty noblemen's and gentlemen's private carriages; and arrived at Burford-bridge at four, from which place, about a mile and a half from Dorking, the body was conveyed in state to the latter town. The cavalcade consisted of the Duke's gentlemen on horseback, fully caparisoned, bearing the ducal coronet and golden batôns of office upon a crimson cushion, before the hearse.

The chief mourners were, the Duke of Norfolk, the Earl of Surrey, Lord Viscount Andover, Henry Howard, jun. esq. and Henry Howard, of Corby Castle, in Cumberland, esq. The gentlemen of the Duke's household, with his servants, followed in six mourning coaches, and the Deputy Garter king of arms, Norroy king of arms, three heralds and three pursuivants, attended in the tabards of state, to perform the ceremonies usual at the funeral of the Earl Marshal of England.

In the mean time, the intense degree of anxiety for the arrival of the procession at Dorking, exceeded all possible conception. The character of the illustrious deceased being so generally known in this neighbourhood, swarms of pedestrians and equestrians poured into the town from all parts of the surrounding country, to view the ceremony.

The long cortège reached Dorking about five o'clock, at the time, when the dusky gloom of evening added to the sombre effect of the melancholy scene; and the attributes of funereal pomp were just seen making up this puny finish of human grandeur :

> So sumptuous, yet so perishing withal!
> * * * * * *
> A thousand mourners deck the pomp of death
> To-day, the breathing marble glows above
> To decorate its memory, and tongues
> Are busy of its life: to-morrow worms
> In silence and in darkness seize their prey.
> *Shelley.*

When arrived at the church-yard gate, the procession was met by the Vicar of Dorking, assisted by the Duke's domestic chaplains: the foot procession was marshalled by the heralds, Norroy king of arms, bearing the coronet.

The church was literally crammed with persons, all anxious to witness the performance of the exequies. After the funeral service, Deputy Garter proclaimed the Duke's style and titles, in the following form and order:

> The Most High, Mighty, and Most Potent Prince,
> Charles Howard, Duke of Norfolk!
> Earl Marshal!
> And Hereditary Earl Marshal of England!
> Earl of Arundel Castle!
> Earl of Surrey! Earl of Norfolk! Earl of Norwich!
> Baron of Mowbray!
> Baron of Howard! Baron of Segrave;
> Baron of Bruvese of Gower!
> Baron Fitz-Alan! Baron Warren! Baron Clun!
> Baron Oswaldestre! Baron Maltravers!
> Baron Greystock! Baron Furnival! Baron Verdon!
> Baron Lovetot! Baron Strange!
> And Premier Baron Howard, of Castle Rising!
> Premier Duke! Premier Earl! Premier Baron of England!
> And Chief of the Illustrious Family of the Howards!

Several coats of arms, pennons, crests, &c. were displayed. The coffin was covered with rich crimson velvet, surmounted with silver ornaments, and the arms were engraven upon a plate of silver gilt, with the following inscription:

> Depositum
> Illustrissimi Principis
> Caroli Howard, Ducis de Norfolk,
> Comitis Mareschalli Angliæ
> Jure Hæreditario;
> Comitis iterum de Arundel et Surrey;
> Baronis de Fitzalan, Clun, Oswaldestre,
> et Maltravers, &c. &c.
> Qui diem obiit supremam
> Die Decemb. XVImo Annoque Sacro
> MDCCCXV.
> Annum agens septuagesimum.

The active life of the late Duke of Norfolk may strictly be termed an interesting epoch in the political history of this country; and has already proved an exhaustless mine of incident, for the biographer and historian. His warm and enthusiastic attachment to the true principles of English liberty, entitled him to unreserved and universal admiration. His exertions in the cause of parliamentary reform, and his zealous co-operation with the leading political characters of his time, to secure that invaluable " birthright," cannot be referred to, without the liveliest emotions of national gratitude to this illustrious nobleman, and his compatriots; however inefficient their efforts have been in accomplishing that salutary measure.

As an agriculturist, and a promoter of the arts and sciences, his vast wealth and possessions enabled him to become an effective member. His plans bore intuitive marks of a strong discriminating mind, which, of course, attached additional importance to his patronage. His rent-roll included an immense number of manors in Nottinghamshire, Yorkshire, Cumberland, Herefordshire, Norfolk, Surrey, and Sussex. Like the late Bishop of Llandaff, he partly employed his recesses from public life, in *Planting;* and we need only recur to the vicinity of Dorking, for records of his useful labours. His manner of living was at once princely and magnificent,—well befitting the character of his august family; and, it is generally thought, that his splendid fête at Arundel Castle, in the June previous to his decease, accelerated that lamentable event. Unhappily, the good old spirit of English hospitality which prevailed at his board, too frequently bordered on injurious excess, which not only embittered real enjoyment, but shortened the course by speedy, if not unexpected, decay.

The habits of the late Duke were truly

eccentric. In his person and dress, he was singularly negligent. When passing through the town of Dorking, with his splendid equipage, he has frequently been known to call and settle the most unimportant business with his tradesmen; and this perhaps with a view, not strictly consistent with his high rank. In short, the life of this illustrious nobleman will, at all times, furnish a rich volume of anecdote—well stored with the sparkling of wit and humour; and, in naiveté and originality of character, far exceeding the career of any of his contemporaries.

Passing by the vestry door, to the churchyard, I noticed the handsome mausoleum of the Talbot family, whose arms are within a pediment at the end, supported by Tuscan columns. From this spot, I enjoyed an uninterrupted view of Box-Hill, Norbury-Park, and Denbies,—the blooming verdure of which seemed to mock the fate of mortals, with whose monuments and memorials I here stood surrounded.

Charitable institutions, and undertakings of public utility, are no-where more liberally supported, or more judiciously conducted, than at Dorking. A zealous spirit of co-operation, unmixed with political or party spirit, pervades the affluent and middle classes of the inhabitants; and the beneficial results of this organized unison are so generally felt and acknowledged, as to render their public establishments, at once, models for various towns and districts throughout the kingdom. The formation and adoption of new systems has, thus, no less occupied the attention of this benevolent community, than the correction of abuses, sanctioned rather by immemorial custom, than by the spirit of the present wise and enlightened age: and the promoters of these salutary measures may now look back on the success of their efforts, during the last five years, with no ordinary feelings of gratification.

PROVIDENT INSTITUTIONS took their rise in this congenial soil. Hence their plan and principles were disseminated abroad, and became the subject of an investigation before a select committee of the House of Commons; and several cities and towns might be quoted, in which the benefits of these establishments have been more or less testified. In considering the prosperity of the Dorking Society, it ought not to be forgotten, that, during five years, upwards of *twelve hundred pounds* have been raised by public subscription for the support of the fund; and that the contributions of the poor subscribers have been proportionally important. The fundamental basis of the system has already been detailed at great length, and ably elucidated, in a statistical point of view, by the Secretary, to whose indefatigable industry may be ascribed its signal success; and whose disinterested services on this as well as on many other public occasions, will at all times be gratefully acknowledged by his fellow-parishioners.*

PUBLIC SCHOOLS, for the education of

---

* The main principle, or key-stone, of this society appears to be in uniting the efforts of the benevolent in one grand scheme, whereby the *poor* might be made *instrumental* in relieving *their own* necessities in seasons of emergency, instead of solely relying on the assistance of the affluent. No scheme can be more conducive to the revival of that spirit of national independence, which the present fallacious system of the poor-laws has tended to repress. In short, the general views of this institution are clearly laid down in the following axioms:

1. "*That no device, or plan, or scheme, be deemed worthy "of the slightest consideration, which has not for its ultimate "object the raising of the poor to a situation, in which they "shall be comparatively independent of adventitious or eleemosy- "nary assistance!*

2. "*That no individual, however humble, can possibly, (whilst "a member of this society,) be doomed to pass the winter months "under the accumulated miseries of cold and hunger; and thus "the* DORKING PROVIDENT INSTITUTION *may fearlessly "be held up as* A GRAND AND PRACTICAL SCHEME FOR "THE SOCIAL AND MORAL IMPROVEMENT OF MANKIND."

Fifth Annual Report, &c.

poor children of both sexes, have, for some time, been established in this parish; and, among their guardians, it is pleasing to observe several ladies of rank and affluence, who are alternately occupied in the inspection and superintendence of the female school. A branch BIBLE SOCIETY, likewise formed some years since, continues to prosecute its important labours in this district, with unwearied diligence. A SAVINGS BANK, countenanced by the whole rank and respectability of the town and adjacent parishes, proffers the usual advantages of such establishments; and which, to judge by its fund, continues to be appreciated by the frugal and industrious classes, for whose interest, savings-banks were originally devised.

In addition to the benefits arising from these institutions, the benevolent dispositions of the gentry of the town and neighbourhood are unceasingly displayed in assisting distressed families or individuals. At stated periods of the year, provisions, fuel, and clothing, are distributed with as much precision, as if bequeathed by will, and perhaps with a much greater regard to the merits of the applicants. A winter of unusual severity never fails to awaken the compassion of the affluent: committees are generally formed for supplying the poor with soup, at reduced prices; and, to those unable to secure the advantages of Provident Institutions, a collateral species of relief is generally afforded.

In truth, the greater part of the improvements which have been accomplished in the several departments of this parish may be traced to the gratuitous agency of a liberal and public-spirited Press. Too much praise cannot, of course, be given to this branch of so effectual an organ of popular opinion; to whose free exercise may be ascribed the whole progress of moral and intellectual improvement during the three last centuries. By disclaiming the virulence of political controversy, many salutary reformations have been made in the conduct of public and parochial affairs. All classes have alike participated in the benefit; and the example of this parish may now be held forth to other districts, as no unimportant proof of the practicability of similar revisions.

The Bank, a substantial stuccoed building, is centrically situate on the left side of the High street.* Opposite, is the Red Lion Inn, which has been much enlarged and improved by its present proprietor. Here was formerly held, a society, called "the Gentlemen's Dorking Club," on every alternate Thursday, from June to November. This inn was likewise a noted house for water-soucey, carp, and perch, which were here served up in great perfection, during the season.

---

* The Reigate bankers have an office in Dorking, and the proprietors of the Dorking Bank have similar accommodations at Reigate and Horsham.

The establishment possesses every comfort and accommodation, which unremitted activity and perseverance can tend to furnish; and the public have been by no means backward in recompensing these efforts with an extensive patronage.

Adjoining the inn, is a chastely-elegant ball-room, lately erected at a very considerable expense. The dimensions are 50 ft. in length; 15 ft. high; and 28 ft. wide. It is tastefully decorated, and fitted up with a small orchestra, and provided with chandeliers, ottomans, couches, &c.

Nearly opposite the entrance, is a door opening to a passage, about 30 ft. in length, cut through a fine sand rock, and communicating by a short flight of steps with a walled garden. The whole is well contrived, and calculated to bring into recollection the magical deceits of Eastern romance;—illusions perhaps sometimes enhanced by the fascinating displays of elegance and beauty, which crowd its avenues! In the garden is an elevated summer-house, or prospect-room, from which the eye at once overlooks the dingy roofs of the town, and regales itself with the several charms of the Deepdene, Box-Hill, Norbury, and Leith-Hill.

The room was opened with a public dinner in the autumn of 1820; and has since been used for balls at the customary season, and on various other occasions. The advantage of so important an addition to public accommodation, reflecting high credit on all parties concerned in its erection, will, of course, be proportionally estimated. Occasional concerts will, at all times, gratify the lovers of music; and public dinners, on occasions of popular festivity, will tend to keep up convivial mirth among those who delight in " the feast of reason and the flow of soul." Dorking will thus present inducements for the *winter resident* as well as the *summer visitor;* and, when divested of its scenic attractions, the pleasures of its well-regulated amusements will, in some degree, compensate for their absence.*

The market-house formerly stood nearly adjoining the Red Lion; but, through neglect, the building fell into a ruinous condition, and at length became a public nuisance. The late Duke of Norfolk, who took great interest in the prosperity of this town, suggested the removal of the unsightly structure, and, it is believed, went so far as to promise

---

* On the left side of the street, also, is the *Wheatsheaf*, a neat public-house, where may be seen an immense hog. The animal, accidentally breaking one of its legs, was killed without fatting; its skin was dressed with the hair on, and is now preserved, stuffed, and standing in full proportion. It exceeded in size the famous Northumberland hog of the year 1543. It weighed 104 stone; or 823 lbs. Its length, 12 feet;—girth, 8 feet;—height, 18 hands: and it is computed, had it been fatted proportionally, it would have weighed nearly 200 stone! This prodigy may be considered well worth the inspection of agriculturists.

the inhabitants a new market-house in its stead. The old building was, accordingly, pulled down; and the materials being sold, the produce, one hundred pounds, was paid to the Duke's agent. The building of the new market-house was delayed for some time; and, the Duke dying in 1815, the inhabitants lost all immediate prospect of the promise being fulfilled. Application was afterwards made to the executors of the late Duke; but, up to this time, no precise arrangement has been made. The fund produced by the sale of the old materials was subsequently divided among the committees for paving the several districts of the town, and it may thus be said to have effected some improvement.

The assizes for the county appear to have been held at Dorking in 1699, but on what occasion is not mentioned. The sessions were likewise formerly held in the Townhall, over the old market-place; but this has not been the case for many years.

An incredible quantity of poultry is usually sold at the weekly markets. This trade is chiefly in the hands of a few individuals, who regularly attend, and supply the London dealers. There is, also, a breed of fowls, with five claws, well known, among the poulterers in the metropolis, by the appellation of "*Dorking fowls*;" one sort is perfectly white, and another of a partridge colour. Columella, in his *Husbandry*, describes fowls of this kind; and it is conjectured that they were originally brought here by the Romans.

Adjoining the site of the market-house, was formerly a massy brick mansion, supposed to have been built from a Dutch model; and, by its extensive proportions, calculated to convey some idea of the importance of its founder. Popular credulity and superstition (strange to say,) had not fixed upon it as the abode of some "evil spirits;" but, through the delay and chicanery of the law, it was, till lately, tenanted only by a widow and her son. The back premises were, likewise, very capacious, and in every respect corresponded with the mansion. This property was sold by auction in 1820; and its purchaser has, at a very great expense, altered the mansion into commodious dwelling-houses, which have a handsome and respectable appearance on entering the town. The prospect from the balconies of the drawing-room windows at once unites the "URBS IN RURE;" and, from the upper story, the *coup-d'œil* of the surrounding country is both cheerful and interesting. The street extending from hence contains some genteel houses, on the left side; and the recently-built line opposite well denotes the public-spirited character of the townsmen in general.*

---

* An important manufactory has lately been established at the back of the town, by Messrs. Burridge, Cluer, and Co. for tanning *Crop Hides*, or *Sole Leather*, in a quarter of the usual time required for that process. These gentlemen have already made affidavits of the above fact. They also state, that the hides tanned by their method are heavier than usual, so that the quality is superior, and some of them have been found to weigh ten or twelve pounds above the raw halves of the hides. This

Dorking, being situate on a sandy rock, abounds with deep and capacious caves or cellars, which are extremely cold, even in the height of summer. The most remarkable of these is one on the left side of Butter-hill, which runs for a considerable distance in an angular direction. On the side of the entrance, is a wide staircase, curiously cut out of the rock, and descending by fifty steps to a crystalline spring of water, which is forty feet perpendicular beneath the entrance cave. About a century ago, an individual expended the whole of his property in digging this cave, and, having thus wasted several hundreds, he is said to have died in the poor-house. The cave is now more profitably used, by a respectable distiller of the town, as a wine cellar,—an appropriation, differing

---

discovery must prove of the most essential benefit to the *tanning-trade*, and indeed to the public at large; as every invention which has for its object, œconomy in so important a necessary as clothing, must, eventually, engage the attention of the whole of the scientific world. Much has already been said and written on the various improvements in the art of tanning during the last few years; and it is cheerfully announced that the desideratum of ages is accomplished by this discovery.

widely from the original design of its projector.

The house, under which this artificial excavation partly extends, was upwards of sixteen years the residence of the Rev. John Mason, chiefly known for his work, entitled "Self-knowledge." Dorking appears to have been the first place, at which the talents of this celebrated dissenting divine were brought into action; for, having completed his education, he accepted the charge of a congregation in this town, where, according to his biographers, he had "a numerous auditory." While at Dorking, he published several works, by which he attained considerable literary reputation, and the degree of M. A. from the Edinburgh University. In the dwelling-house above mentioned, Mr. Mason completed his well known "Treatise on Self-knowledge," a work "full of sense and sentiment," and which has, perhaps, done more towards the formation of sound opinions on that important science, than any contemporary publication; while, in point of purity of style and literary merit, it may be held up as a work displaying much erudition and profound research. It has been translated into several European languages, has long ranked high as a British classic, and forms a truly valuable source of elegant and instructive reading for youth of both sexes.

Mr. Mason quitted this town in July, 1746, for Cheshunt, in Hertfordshire, and was afterwards engaged in the publication of several theological works. He also directed his attention to the study of the belles lettres, and, in this department, he produced an "Essay on Elocution," which rapidly passed through several editions, and became a popular text-book in one of the English Universities.

On leaving the town of Dorking, I passed Shrub-Hill, upwards of twenty-five years the residence of the late EARL of Rothes, and subsequently of the dowager Countess. Here the Earl and his amiable family entertained her Majesty Queen Charlotte, at a sumptuous dejeuné, on her return from Brighton to Windsor, in 1816; for which mark of loyalty and attachment, the Queen was afterwards pleased to express herself in terms of the highest approbation.

The following biographical notice of this family, collected from various authentic sources, may not perhaps prove uninteresting to the general reader.

The Leslies, now nearly at the head of the Earls in the Scottish peerage, are of a very ancient family and high descent. They were of foreign origin; and the first of that name in Great Britain was Bartholdus Lesley, one of the Hungarian *Magnates*, who, in the year 1086, attended Margaret Atheling, the wife of King Malcolm Canmore, into Scotland. There his merits, in addition to his services to that princess, were deemed so considerable, that King Malcolm gave him his own sister in marriage; and, besides many large possessions, made him Governor of Edinburgh Castle, a place which, under his management became of the highest consequence to the reigning family. From him descended George Leslie, created Lord Leslie, Earl of Rothes, by James II. in 1457.

By another writer it is stated that Bartholomew de Leslyn possessed the barony of Leslyn, in Aberdeenshire, so early as 1165; and that his descendant, George, was honoured with the earldom alluded to above; but that the precise date is uncertain, being between the years 1455 and 1459. William, the third Earl, lost his life at the fatal battle of Flodden-field; and his eldest son, George, appears to have been one of those zealous reformers, who, in 1546, seized on the castle of Cardinal Beaton at St. Andrew's.

The fourth Earl of Rothes attended Queen Mary to France, in order to be espoused by the Dauphin; John, the sixth Earl, joined the Covenanters; but, being one of the deputies from Scotland to Charles I., then in captivity, was gained over, according to Burnet, by the hopes of marrying the "Countess of Devonshire, a rich and magnificent lady."

His son John fought for Charles II. at Worcester, and returned with the King after his exile. His favour now became preponderant at court, for he was Lord High Treasurer, Lord Keeper of the Great Seal, Lord Chancellor, &c. Dr. Burnet says, " the King loved him, though it was a very extravagant thing to see one man possess so many of the chief places of so poor a kingdom." In 1680, he was created Duke of Rothes, Marquis of Ballinbreach and Cuskieberrie; but, as his Grace died without male issue, the patent, in consequence of the limitations, expired with himself.

Margaret, the eldest daughter, having married Charles Hamilton, the fifth Earl of Haddington, their son John became the eighth Earl of Rothes. On the accession of George I. he was appointed Lord High Admiral of Scotland, and died in 1722. John, the ninth Earl, was a Lieutenant-General, and had a regiment of guards, and his only son John, dying in 1778 without male issue, was succeeded by his eldest sister.

George William Evelyn Leslie, the eleventh earl of Rothes, was the son of George Raymond Evelyn, Esq. by Jane-Elizabeth Countess of Rothes. He was born March 28, 1768, and, after receiving the usual education, settled in England, where he married twice. His first wife was Lady Henrietta-Anna Pelham, eldest daughter of Thomas Earl of Chichester; with this lady, to whom he became united in May 24, 1789, he had no male issue; there were, however, three daughters, viz. Henrietta-Anne, Amelia*, and Mary. The Countess dying on December 5th, 1797, in August 1798 his lordship espoused Charlotte-Julia, daughter of Colonel John Campbell, of Dunoon; and here also there were no male children, but two females, Elizabeth-Jane and Georgiana, the latter of whom is since dead.

In 1810, the Earl of Rothes succeeded to the titles, and some estates still vested in the family; among which is the *Seignory* of Rothes, a lordship on the banks of the Spey, a few miles distant from Elgin in the county of Morey. His lordship, however, never lived in Scotland, as he preferred his delightful retreat at Shrub-Hill.

The death of the Earl took place on

---

*Lady Amelia Leslie died at Long Ditton, a few days after the demise of her father. His eldest daughter, Lady Henrietta, who became Countess of Rothes on the death of the Earl, died in 1820.

the 21st of February, 1817, attended with the following extraordinary circumstances. In the afternoon of that day, his Lordship left Shrub-Hill to join some brother sportsmen in the chase: after riding a short time, his Lordship descried them in Betchworth Park; and, shortly after reaching them, was heard to say he was unwell. The alarm soon spread, and the noble Earl was conveyed to Betchworth Castle, where, after a short struggle, he expired! In the mean time an express had been sent to Dorking, for medical assistance, but its arrival proved useless. The melancholy news speedily became circulated in all directions, and the intense degree of public sympathy excited by this distressing event, exceeds all possible description.

As a legislator, the Earl of Rothes was not prominent; he, however, in his character of one of the sixteen peers of Scotland, seconded the dutiful and respectful address which was moved at the opening of parliament in 1817, and acquitted himself with a considerable share of ability on that occasion.

The dowager-Countess, and her daughters, the Ladies Mary and Elizabeth-Jane Leslie, still reside at Shrub-Hill, where they enjoy the first society which this opulent and extensive neighbourhood possesses. They are here enabled to support a comfortable, but unostentatious establishment; and, in this rural retirement, they, doubtless, find a happy retreat from the vicissitudes and perplexities of public life.

As a patroness of the several institutions in this parish, the Countess has proved herself a zealous supporter of the interests of all classes: and, in these acts of pure benevolence, her ladyship is uniformly joined by her amiable daughters; —thus presenting inestimable patterns of moral excellence united with all its characteristic accomplishments.

The pleasure-grounds of Shrub-Hill

England." The spot has also long been proverbial in the country for the superiority of its situation. The name signifies, in our ancient language, " the heath of poor cottages." In the survey of 1649, it is said to contain 15¼ acres,* but this has, doubtless, been contracted by encroachments.

Cotmandene is backed by the rising foliage of the woods and plantations of the Deepdene; and, overlooking the town, it possesses fine prospects of the surrounding country. On its borders are a few neat residences, several small cottages, and a row of alms-houses, occupied by aged and infirm poor, who receive a small stipend from the endowed funds. Matches of cricket are often decided here in the summer season ; and, on such occasions, this beautiful area

---

* Salmon, as it will be seen before, mentions it as containing twenty acres.

usually presents a truly animated picture of mirth and pastime.

The neighbourhood of Dorking has long been noted for the salubrity of the air, and the picturesque beauty of its scenery: a short residence here is frequently recommended to invalids, by London medical practitioners, and is generally attended with speedy convalescence, or essential benefit. Physicians are, also, of opinion, that the alkaline properties of the chalk-hills, in the vicinity, are highly conducive to the health of the resident population; an opinion, which is, in some degree, corroborated by the numerous visitors who resort hither at the most favourable periods of the year.

In summer, the town and its environs are usually thronged with company, and lodgings are in great request. In the year 1798, Dr. Aikin was a resident here, for the benefit of his health; and in the Monthly Magazine, he has given a short description of this country, which he concluded with the following apposite remarks:

"It would be easy to enlarge the beautiful scenes in this neighbourhood, all within the reach of a morning's walk or ride, and affording a source of daily variety for several weeks. The purity of the air, the fragrance from an exuberance of aromatic plants and shrubs, the music from the numberless birds, the choice of sheltered or open country, the liberty of wandering without obstacles or questions through the most cultured scenes, and the perfect repose which reigns all round, unite to render this tract of country one of the most delightful to the contemplative man, and the most salutary to the invalid, that I have ever visited." J. A.

The view of the town from Cotmandene presents an assemblage of buildings in every style, from the ponderous old roof to the elegant and modern parapet wall. There are few mansions in the streets, but their general appearance may be said to be above the *mediocre*. There are also several compact cottages in the environs, which unite neatness of exterior with the genuine English charm of snugness and comfort. The whole parish, according to the census of last year, contained 697 houses, occupied by 842 families. At that period, also, there were 14 houses building, and 30 uninhabited.

In 1801, the population consisted of 3058 persons,—and, in 1811, of 3259.

The following is an authentic abstract of the Returns of Population, taken in July, 1821:—the increase being 553.

OCCUPATIONS.			Persons, including Children of whatever age.		
Families chiefly employed in Agriculture.	Families chiefly employed in Trade, Manufactures, and Handicraft.	All other families not comprised in the two preceding classes.	Males. No.	Females. No.	Total of Persons.
308	335	199	1878	1934	3812

Pauperism, however, seems to have made rapid strides with the increase of population. The poor-rates were

In 1642—*three-pence* in the pound;
In 1670—*one-shilling* in the pound;
In 1787—*three shillings* in the pound;

and, in 1817, they amounted to the enormous sum of *eight shillings* in the pound—an evil which has been in some degree lessened by the united efforts of Provident Institutions, and a course of rigid œconomy in the expenditure of the parish funds—a measure as essential to *parochial* prosperity, as to *national* greatness; and the policy of which must ultimately find its way into the antiquated systems of parochial jurisprudence, and the councils of wise and temperate rulers, notwithstanding its promoters may for a time have to combat with the scepticism and prejudices engendered by custom and rote.

From Cotmandene, I passed by an obscure path, overlooking the gardens and premises at the back of the south side of the High-street; and, after a few minutes' walk, I reached the park-like grounds of *Rose-Hill*, the property of Richard Lowndes, esq. The residence, a commodiously-built mansion, is placed at a short distance from the thoroughfare. In its immediate vicinity are some extensive gardens, tastefully laid out, and communicating with a shrubbery, by several serpentine walks. The spacious drawing-room at the back opens on a beautiful lawn, and possesses a pleasant prospect over the adjacent fields and meadows. At the extremity of the park or paddock, is a retired gravelled walk, overshaded by a line of thick firs, and forming a cool and agreeable retreat during the summer. After a short walk across the fields, I arrived at the southern extremity of the town, where I noticed several neat dwelling-houses, particularly a handsome stuccoed residence, belonging to Thomas Stilwell, esq. Proceeding by a circuitous route through a shady lane, I arrived at the end of West-street: from hence, westward, is the lower road to Guildford, at the angle of which is *Sand-Place*, (alias Sond-Place,) the ancient residence of the family of Sondes, from which they, probably, took their name. This estate is now in the possession of Hugh Bishopp, esq. of the De-la-Zouch family.

The house is placed on a high sand-bank, and screened from the road by a stone wall. The gardens and grounds, which are very limited, are disposed of with great taste and advantage.

Leaving the road, I crossed a hilly field on the left, with a view of visiting *Milton-Court*, a spacious and substantial farm-house, which appears, by the style of building, to have been erected in the reign of Queen Elizabeth.* Hither, that excellent scholar and critic, JEREMIAH MARKLAND, passed the last twenty-four years of his life. "In 1752," his pupil, Mr. Strode, says, "being grown old, and having, moreover, long and painful fits of the gout, he was glad to find, what his inclination and infirmities, which made

---

* The mill, adjoining the green before the mansion, is supposed to be the one mentioned in Domesday book, in the particulars of the manor of Milton.

him unfit for the world and company, had for a long time led him to,—a very private place of retirement, near Dorking, in Surrey." In this pleasant and sequestered spot, Markland saw little company. His walks were almost confined to the narrow limits of the garden at the back of the house; and he described himself, in 1755, to be "as much out of the way of hearing, as of getting." What first induced him to retire is not precisely known, but it is conjectured to have originated in some disappointment of a private nature.

The retirement of Markland from public life may, however, be considered as having been highly congenial to his favourite pursuits. He was constantly engaged in writing notes and emendations for improved editions of some of the first Greek classics; in which task he manifested high qualifications, both as an erudite scholar and impartial critic.

In 1765, a circumstance occurred,

which will long reflect a lustre on the character of this important luminary of classical literature. The widow with whom he lodged, at Milton-Court, became involved in a family litigation, by the injustice and oppression of her son, who persuaded her to assign to him the whole of her property.* Mr. Markland, in defending the cause of the widow, expended a considerable sum, and, the case being decided against her, he benevolently employed his fortune in relieving the dis-

---

* My engaging in a law matter was much contrary to my nature and inclination, and owing to nothing but compassion, (you give it a suspicious name when you call it tenderness; she being in her 63d year, and I in my 74th,) to see a worthy woman oppressed and deprived by her own son of every farthing she had in the world, and nothing left to subsist herself and two children, but what she received from me for board and lodging; and this too endeavoured by several bad and ridiculous methods to be taken from her, and myself forced hence, that they might compel her into their unjust measures; not to mention the lesser injuries, indignities, and insolences, which were used towards her. Could I run away, and leave an afflicted good woman and her children to starve, without the greatest baseness, dishonour, and inhumanity? Poor as I am, I would rather have pawned the coat on my back than have done it. I speak this in the presence of God: and I appeal to Him before whom I must soon appear, that this is the true and only reason of my acting in this matter; and, though I know that the consequences of it will incommode me greatly, and almost ruin me, yet I am sure I shall never repent it.
Letter from Mr. Markland, in Nichols's Bowyer.

tresses of the family. The independence of his mind induced him to refuse several honourable offers of assistance from his friends, and, with the greatest reluctance, he was at last prevailed upon to accept a small annuity from one of his former pupils.

Repeated attacks of the gout, and an accumulation of infirmities, at length put an end to his life, at Milton-Court, in July 1776, in the eighty-third year of his age. He bequeathed his books and papers to Dr. Heberden, and his other property to Mrs. Rose, the widow, whose cause he had so honourably supported in his life-time. His funeral was performed agreeably to his own request, in the chancel of Dorking church, where a small brass plate commemorates his learning and virtue. His books were valuable, from the manuscript notes which they contained; and, on the death of his friend Dr. Heberden, they fell into the hands of different eminent literary men.

"It is to be regretted," says his biographer, "that the splendour of Markland's abilities was obscured by the extreme privacy of his life, and the many peculiarities of his disposition. His frequent despondency was, in some measure, also produced by his interesting himself too much in the politics of the time, which he always viewed through a gloomy medium.

The most conspicuous trait in his character was his singular and unwearied industry. His long life was chiefly passed in collating the classic authors of antiquity, and illustrating the book of Revelation; and, even in his eighty-first year, he is said to have displayed proofs of vigour and clearness of intellect, perfectly astonishing at that protracted season of life. For modesty, candour, literary honesty, and courteousness to other scholars, he was not only considered the most accomplished man of his time; but he is to this day ranked as the model which ought to be proposed for the imitation of every critic ; while his valuable and important contributions to the general stock of classical lore cannot fail to render his memory highly interesting to all engaged in its refined pursuits.

The spacious rooms of Milton-Court, with their long polished tables and benches, served strongly to remind me of the hospitality of former times. We certainly have not but few of these venerable mansions, whose blazing hearths shed a hospitable glare along the carved walls, and, shining through their windows, invited those who passed, to partake of the good cheer which reigned within. In this respect, we have left only the *shadow* for the substance; or, as aptly observed by a periodical writer, "what the present race have gained in head, they have lost in heart."

A visit to Milton-Court cannot fail to resuscitate similar emotions of regret ; and, doubtless, several of my contemporaries will recognize in its lofty hall, the scene of many a jocund hour, unmixed with the forms and ceremonies of more recent introduction. Frequently have I heard them recur to those hours; and I can well depict to myself the harmless " gambols on the green;" the overflowing mirth of the harvest-home; the cheerfulness and vivacity of the dance; and the moon-light walk across the fields. Alas! how changed the scene! Aggravated distresses have partially set aside the celebration of the harvest-home; and the dances to commemorate the festive season of the year. Where now is the smiling host, welcoming to his board whole groupes of healthful youth and beauty! Where now is the annual boon to those swarms of industrious peasantry, with their hearts brim-full of gladness!

"When loose to festive joy, the country round
"Laughs with the loud sincerity of mirth."
Thomson.

Surely, they all appear but to have been

the mere delusions of some idle hour: be this as it may, their absence has left a chasm in the unsophisticated enjoyments of country life, which after-times have as yet been unable to supply.¹

About half a mile from Dorking, on the Guildford road, is the manor of *Milton*, the antient and proper name of which is Middleton, (written in Domesday book " Mildeton,") and is supposed to have been so called from lying midway between the manors of Dorking and Westcott. By the same record, also, it appears to have been a manor before the Norman Conquest. In 1599, it was granted by Queen Elizabeth to George Evelyn, Esq. from whom it has been transmitted to the successive representatives of that antient family.

Passing over *Milton-Heath*, on the north side of the road may be observed a considerable mound of earth, which, upon inspection is circular and flat at the top; and has the appearance of having been artificially thrown up. It is not unlikely that this is one of the monuments of the primitive inhabitants of this country, called a barrow, which they threw up over their dead. There are, also, some facts, which tend to confirm this idea. A field, on Milton-Court farm, a short distance westward from this mound and adjoining the high road, is called War Field, and the inhabitants in this neighbourhood have a tradition it was so called from a battle having been fought there. This, however, is not supported by historical record, and the only circumstance to add strength to this tradition is, the neighbouring estate being called Bury-Hill, as is conjectured from the Saxon Burʒ, a camp or fort, for which the situation is well adapted.

On the left of the road, is a carriage-drive to *Bury-Hill*, the estate of Robert Barclay, esq. The road is pleasantly overhung with trees, and, extending along the side of the hill, affords an interesting view of the respective hamlets of Westcott and Milton, while, at a short distance, is seen the town of Dorking, with all its circumjacent beauties.

The original proprietor of this estate was Edward Walter, esq. (grandson and heir of Peter Walter, esq. a Dorsetshire gentleman,) who, accidentally seeing this country, was so pleased with it, that he bought a farm, called *Chardhurst*, and several other lands in the neighbourhood of Bury-Hill. He occasionally resided at the house on Chardhurst, during the building of the mansion at Bury-Hill; and, in that house, he was married by special licence to Harriet, the youngest daughter of George, Lord Forrester.

Mr. Walter also made great purchases in Dorking, and soon became the principal landed proprietor in the parish. He resided at Bury-Hill, until his death in 1780: he left one daughter, who, in 1774, married Viscount Grimston, created a peer of Great Britain in 1790, by the title of Baron Verulam. She inherited this estate, and died in 1787, leaving one son, James Walter Grimston, the present Lord Verulam, who, upon his father's decease, succeeded to the estates of Mr. Walter. His lordship has since sold the whole of these estates, with the exception of the great tythes of the parish, to various persons. The Bury-Hill estate, together with several farms, &c. were purchased by Robert Barclay, esq. the present proprietor.

After the death of Mr. Walter, the mansion was occupied by James Richardson, esq. and subsequently by G. Shum, esq. Mr. Barclay first came in 1805.

The eminence on the north side of the mansion was inclosed by Mr. Walter from the waste of Milton manor. He also planted it chiefly with Scotch firs, which have flourished so well, that many good trees have already been cut for timber. The hill on the east of the plantation, belongs to this estate, and is called the

Nower: on its crest is a small summer-house, commanding an extensive prospect, diversified with hill and dale.

A smaller *cordon* of paling incloses the hill, sloping in all directions, and descending to a beautiful terrace-walk, and, at length, to the back-front of the residence, by a fine shelving lawn.

The mansion is both elegant and commodious, and the offices are planned on an extensive scale. Comfort and compactness seem no less to have directed the attention of the architect, than a due regard to neatness and symmetrical beauty. All superfluous ornament is entirely dispensed with, and its absence is made up by uniformity and good taste. The whole is stuccoed, and has been considerably improved by Mr. Barclay.

Beyond the mansion, the land still stretches away in a gentle descent to the edge of an extensive sheet of water, with a small island in its centre, planted with trees and shrubs; and, beyond the whole, are the woods and groves of *Anstiebury*, and a rich and variegated expanse of forest scenery.

The general aspect of this estate is that of genuine and unadorned rusticity, without any of those costly elegancies and embellishments, (so called,) which often tend to divest Nature of her sweetest charms. The artificial sheet of water in the front of the mansion, is judiciously managed, so as to bear the semblance of a river; while its stream bathes a grassy bank, along which a broad gravelled walk runs in a curvilinear direction from the house, and opens by an elegant iron gate to the farm-lands. Besides this, no attempt has been made in the way of ornament, except two or three summer-houses, whose simple and unostentatious structure reminds the pedestrian that they are merely placed there for his temporary accommodation, and to assist him in descrying the several beauties of the surrounding country.

The grounds every-where present successions of beautiful verdant slopes, and walks winding over the fir-crowned summits of the hills, in many parts, leading through spots, full of characteristic and romantic wildness. Nothing can be finer than the ascent up the furzy sides of the hill, by rugged flights of steps, beaten by frequent visitors, and extending under the shade of spreading and aged oaks and beeches; and at length leading to a thick grove of firs, whose sombre branches throw around them an air of melancholy, though not unpleasing, gloominess. At the extremity of this grove, several cheerful walks through flourishing plantations, present a lively contrast, and, after wandering through scenes of exquisite sylvan beauty, burst forth on a picturesque view, full of new objects to engage the ideas of the contemplative pedestrian. In another part, the paths unite with walks, formed by tastefully-arranged flower-borders, overlooking the rich valley beneath, at length terminated by bold eminences, thickly clothed with wood, and "distinguished by those interesting appellations, which make us seek, in our walks, the very foot-marks of the Roman soldier."

On the borders of the grounds, are several cottages. One of them, on the north side of the hill, was formerly an aviary, but has been altered into a school for girls, which is supported at the private expence of the Misses Barclay, who alternately superintend the establishment. The lodges at the different gates are not those stiff and formal buildings, which frequently present such obvious incongruities on similar estates. On the contrary, they are uniform specimens of rural neatness, which feature invariably denotes the exemplary effects of this discipline on the characters of their inmates.

Such are the scenes of rural simplicity which Bury-Hill presents. They cannot fail to please infinitely more than all the fastidious disposal of the choicest flower-gardens; and, after the eye has feasted itself with those multicoloured scenes, the effect becomes doubly pleasing. Even the ruinous hovel, or the meanest cottage, has then charms of no ordinary gratification. Here, also, the rude track of an agricultural cart or waggon, and the sheep and cows pasturing in the valley beneath the woody heights, served to indicate the appropriation of these grounds to the more useful purposes of farming.

Mr. Barclay and his family present a happy groupe, whose members are constantly employed in deeds of pure philanthropy and benevolence. Their individual merits have already been made known to the public, by a celebrated living authoress, in a publication of acknowledged and deserved repute. Fidelity and accuracy of detail have rendered her sketch of this amiable family, one of the most striking examples of knowledge of men and manners, and superior descriptive skill, to be met with in the whole of her writings. Equal in effect to the most exquisite touches in a highly-finished portrait, no person, possessing the slightest knowledge of this family, can fail to recognize, in the "HILBURY" and "Mr. FRANKLAND" of her description, the delightful estate of Bury-hill, and its present worthy proprietor; and it may safely be said that the chapter of which they form the joint subjects, will be found to be equal, in interest and aptitude of delineation, to the ordinary contents of the volume. After this direct allusion, it would be indelicate, and perhaps unnecessary to *name* the authoress, or the production itself. Popular discernment has already attached a considerable share of approbation to the work; and, while useful and important instruction continue to be conveyed in such elegant and well-executed sketches of *real life*, we trust these and all similar qualifications will not fail in meeting with their due encouragement.

Mr. Barclay is well known as a strenuous promoter of the interests of our best and dearest institutions—national, county, and parochial; and, in their success, his sanction is not merely nominal, but is materially enhanced by a series of unwearied exertions. In these philanthropic undertakings, Mr. B. is joined by the whole of his family, who are uniformly influenced by his paternal example, both in pecuniary liberality and operative services. The same spirit of beneficence seems to pervade each member of this family; and, thus acting in heavenly concert, they present a picture of pure and disinterested zeal for the extension of the comforts and happiness of their fellow-creatures.

The exertions of this benevolent circle are not, however, confined to acts of *public* charity. There are few, in their neighbourhood, that cannot bear grateful testimony to their *private* beneficence, limited only by the necessities of the case, to which their attention is directed; and it is not too much to say, that, they annually dispense a handsome fortune, in this prudent system of relieving the casualties and calamities of their needy neighbours.

Mr. Barclay possesses considerable knowledge and taste in the study of botany; and his extensive gardens, in the neighbourhood, abound with many choice plants and exotics. As a practical and experimental agriculturist, his talents are ranked high among the farmers of Surrey; and his generosity in supporting the interests of that honourable class of the community, is strictly proportionate with the other features of his patriotic character.

Mr. B. is on terms of intimacy with the benevolent Mrs. Fry, Mr. Buxton, and several other public characters, whose efforts in improving our present system of *prison discipline* will long be recorded; and, in co-operating with those worthy individuals, Mr. B. alone proves himself a sincere and warm-hearted philanthropist.

Mr. Barclay is a lineal descendant of Robert Barclay,* the celebrated apologist for the Quakers; and consequently of an antient and very honourable family. His sons are well known in the metropolis, one as an active partner in the extensive brewery concern, of which his father is the principal; and the other as a merchant in the city.†

Leaving Bury-Hill, I strolled through

---

* This gentleman died at Urie in 1690, leaving seven children; the last survivor, Mr. David Barclay, a merchant of London, had the singular honour of receiving at his house, in Cheapside, three successive kings, George I. II. and III. when, at their accession, they favoured the city with their presence. From his windows they witnessed the procession, previous to their dining with the Lord-Mayor and Corporation at Guildhall, on Lord-Mayor's day.

† The names of these gentlemen will, also, be found in the official lists of many charitable societies in London, either as presidents, vice-presidents, or co-operative

G

the pleasant hamlet of *Milton*. Here I noticed several small cottages, presenting perfect patterns of cleanliness and comfort. Each of these dwellings was fronted by a small piece of ground, well stocked with flowers, and laid out in beds, evidently with much œconomy.

A low wicket opened on a cleanly-swept gravelled path, edged with box, and leading to the door, on each side of which were some flowering twigs entwining round the trunks of trees; while along the walls stretched the luxuriant leafiness of the grape-vine, whose shoots grew over the window's edge, and partially blinded its panes.* From the flower-beds, here and there might be seen the sweet-briar and the rose-tree:

---

members of the committees; and, in the discharge of their duties, they evince the same public-spirited character, for which their family have been so long and justly celebrated.

* The soil of Dorking and its neighbourhood is highly congenial to the growth of grape-vines. Hence almost every house in this part has its vine; and some of them

there, also, was the daisied border, spotted with gorgeous pionies, and variegated with tufts of pinks, or hearts-ease. In the midst of this motley assemblage rose the fantastically-clipped holly-bush, or the spreading old apple-tree. In another part, were beds of healthy vegetables, interspersed with gooseberry-bushes and currant-trees; and in a remote corner might be seen a rural bower, formed by honeysuckles and jessamines, entwining round osiers or rude lattice-work.

Scarcely an inch of ground could be seen which was not appropriated to some useful or ornamental purpose, alike serving to indicate the assiduity of its owner, and furnishing a continued source of profitable employment for his leisure hours.

---

are very productive. The cottages of the labouring poor are not without this ornament, and the produce is usually sold by them to their wealthier neighbours, for the manufacture of wine. The price per bushel is from 4s. to 16s.; but the variableness of the season frequently disappoints them in the crops, the produce of which is usually laid up as a set-off to the payment of rent.

In these scenes of *cottage* happiness, HOGARTH might have found a model for his "Cottage of Industry," since every object so strictly accords with the simplicity and well-turned satire of that masterly sketch.*

In Milton-street I also noticed the kitchen-gardens, &c. belonging to the

---

* A parting glimpse of these peaceful abodes drew my attention to the condition of their inmates. One of them I found to be a labourer with a family of children, whose average wages were from 14s. to 16s. per week. On this scanty pittance no fewer than eight individuals relied for sustenance, a disproportion attributable to the present unprecedented depression in agricultural affairs. Frugality and forbearance are the only means by which he can wrest himself from the degradation of the workhouse, or the acceptance of parochial relief! A rigid course of housewifery places the character of his mistress in a light which forms a model for her sex, in the judicious management of domestic affairs. It is thus the benign qualities of woman shine forth with unrivalled lustre, impart to man in smiles of cheerfulness and vivacity the unalloyed transports of connubial bliss, and prove a specific solace in the gloomy hour of woe. Sweet sample of unspotted innocence! how often does the hand of private beneficence descend from the paternal mansion to minister to thy wants and necessities! and how often does

Bury-Hill establishment. Crossing a narrow brook by a wooden bridge, I followed a pleasant walk by some hilly fields, which overlook Milton and the neighbouring estate. I soon reached the hamlet of *Westcott*, which may be said to unite all the charms of rural quiet, with singular gentility, and neatness of appearance. The manor, which is of great antiquity, is on record before the Conquest, and was held by Ralph de Felgeres, one of the followers of the Conqueror from Normandy. The hamlet contains a few cottage-residences, built in the modern style, and chiefly occupied by wealthy farmers.

Enquiring for a spot of ground, noted as once having been the site of an antient castle, I was referred to an obscure farm-

---

the charitable zeal of amiable benefactresses exhort thee by personal bounty, when drooping under sickness or misfortune. Such meritorious acts of benevolence prove how incompatible with true charity, are the misapplied means of fashionable almsgiving.

house, in the neighbourhood, for some information on this subject. My guide led me to a square piece of ground, containing about a quarter of an acre, enclosed by a high bank, which is evidently artificial. The old gentleman assured me that for several years past the adjoining field had been known by the name of " Castle Field" and " Castle Meadow." Some ruins have been dug up from the spot, in order to convert it to a kitchen-garden, and, accordingly, it has since been called " Castle Garden."

Thus, it seems probable that there was formerly a castle in the parish of Dorking. Aubrey speaks of two castles, by the names of Denham and Blackhawes, and the above are the only authenticated facts which can be construed into a tradition relating to either of them. The speculations and conjectures of antiquarians on this subject have been both numerous and contradictory. Gough, in his " Additions to Camden," says, " over against Dorking Church, in a meadow, called *Benham-Castle Meadow*, is the moat of a castle, supposed to have been destroyed by the Danes."

I found my guide pretty conversant as to *supposition*, but, "his memory failing him," he could afford me no further information as to the identity of the spot. I accordingly thanked the accommodating old gentleman for his attention, and returned to Westcott Street. Here the *coup d'œil* of the road, the smoke curling between the trees, and the entrance to the retired lanes, corresponded with the pleasing features of village-scenery. Groupes of lively children, sporting on the flowery banks, were emblems of health and innocence, and broke the silence with their harmless prattle. However ominous this simplicity might appear, it was in unison with the general deportment of these villagers, among whom scarcely a dissolute character could be found. Crime, with all its rapid strides, had as yet left them incorrupt; and, notwithstanding the grievances of unrequited labour, the mal-practices of filching and plundering of property could be traced only in a few instances.

Ascending *Westcott Hill*, on the left is a genteel farm-house ; and, adjoining, is the neat residence of Mrs. Hibbert; where, looking over the hedge, I espied the retired gardens, corresponding in tasteful display with the rusticated *cottage-orné*.

On the crest of the hill is a small bench, from which spot the prospect is truly grand and imposing, and such as cannot fail to interest and amuse the wearied pedestrian.

On the left are the thickly-wooded heights of Bury-Hill, whose sombre tints present a bold and vigorous fore-ground. Beyond Bury-Hill is seen the joyful foliage of the Deepdene woods, almost environing the stately mansion ; here rising in amphitheatrical ridges, and there sinking into deep glens and receding like the shades in a highly-finished painting. The barren and cheerless aspect of Brockham-Hill succeeds this luxuriant display of sylvan beauty; while its venerable neighbour, Box-Hill, presents a rugged and frightful precipice, interspersed with its *viretum*, and rivalled only by the far-famed enchantments of Norbury Park, and the blooming verdure of Denbies and the Ranmer hills.

The valley displays a scene, no less interesting, though varying in its character. The furzy ruggedness of Westcot-Heath descends, by numerous sandy roads and bye paths, to the delightful little hamlet, beyond which, the road winds over Milton-Heath to the town of Dorking, with the picturesque country of Mickleham and Letherhead at the extremity of the view.

By a single turn of the head, this beautiful *panorama* of Nature is completed, with "the Rookery," and the undulating fields and meadows in the neighbourhood, terminated by the winding perspective of the road, formed by high sand-banks, and overhung with flourishing hedges.

Nothing could have exceeded the exhilarating effects of this scene. The advancing day seemed to usher in additional beauties, and exhibit the richness of the prospect with increased vigour. The trees waved their branches to the playful breezes; the notes of innumerable birds resounded in the thickets; and the lark was still carolling her song with all the sweet expressiveness of devotional ardour. The poetic features of this spot would furnish many happy subjects for the pastorals and sonnets of BLOOMFIELD, or the unstudied effusions of CLARE— whose muses can well delineate the artlessness of rural life in all the feeling fluency of melody and rhyme. Every one must acknowledge the effect of sublime scenery on the mind and heart, and he who but once feels the genial glow it creates, will court more frequent interviews with this fascinating country.

Descending from Westcott-Hill, I passed the gate of the carriage-drive to the Rookery, and crossed the stream by a plank bridge. A curious stone wall also extends across the stream, and the current, running through three arches over several crags, gives it the appearance of a miniature cascade.

After a short walk through the fields, I passed the Wotton rectory, a neat brick edifice, delightfully placed in the valley, and considerably improved and enlarged by its respective occupants. The grounds and gardens contiguous to the house, are very limited, but evince much taste in the arrangement. The present incumbent is the Hon. and Rev. John Evelyn Boscawen, brother to Viscount Falmouth.

A short distance from hence, is Wotton Church, consisting of various orders of building, both antient and modern. It is placed on a knoll, and embosomed in full-grown trees, so as to render its spire scarcely perceptible in the approach. The interior contains several monuments, among which are two neat tablets, denoting the burial-place of the Earl of Rothes, and the deceased members of the family. The one to the memory of his lordship bears the following inscription:

To the memory of
George William, Earl of Rothes,
Baron Leslie of Bambreigh,
(son of George Raymond Evelyn, Esq. and
Jane-Elizabeth Leslie, Countess of Rothes
in her own right, whom he succeeded in 1809;)
one of the sixteen Peers of Scotland,
born March 23, 1768,
died February 11, 1817.

Praised be thy memory! honor'd be thy tomb!
Bless'd be thy spirit in a world to come:
Able he was, affectionate and just,
  In every character of life rever'd;
True to his king, attentive to his trust,
  By social virtues to his friends endeared.

With judg'ment sound, with understanding clear,
  One steady line of conduct he pursued;
With heart untainted, as with tongue sincere,
  He won the friendship of the wise and good.

His manners were by graceful taste adorn'd,
  His conversation was by sense inspir'd;
In death he universally is mourn'd,
  As he in life was honor'd and admir'd.

His afflicted widow, and once happy wife, inscribes this marble, an unequal testimony of his worth and excellence, and his affection; wishing that heaven to her may grace supply.

A handsome tablet, on the opposite side, presents a contrast with the bare whitewashed walls, and serves to denote the vault of the antient family of the Steeres, at Ockley.

About one hundred and sixty years ago, as some workmen were digging in the church-yard, they found an entire skeleton, which, on being measured with a pole, proved to be 9 ft. 8 inches long. It was lying between two boards of the coffin; but, on the workmen endeavouring to take it out, it fell to pieces. In the north aisle of the chancel is the dormitory of the EVELYNS. It is enclosed with wooden balustrades; and the tablets and devices are in the antique style. The celebrated philosopher, JOHN EVELYN, is interred here in a stone coffin; and the following transcript of his epitaph may probably afford some interest to the curious reader.

Here lies the Body of
JOHN EVELYN, Esq.;
who having served y^e publick
in several employments, of which that
of Commissioner of y^e privy seal, in the
Reign of King James y^e 2nd. was most
honourable, & perpetuated his fame
by far more lasting monuments than
those of stone or brass; his learned
and usefull works fell asleep y^e 27th day
of Feb. 170$\frac{5}{6}$, being y^e 86th year
of his age, in full hope of a glorious
resurrection thro' faith in Jesus Christ.
Living in an age of extraordinary
events & revolutions, he learn't
(as himself asserted) this truth,
which pursuant to his intention
is here declared—*That all is vanity wch is not honest;*
and there 's no solid wisdom
but in real piety.

Of five sons & three daughters
borne to him from his most vertuous & excellent wife,
Mary, sole daughter and heiress

of Sr Rich. Browne, of Sayes
Court, near Deptford in Kent,
onely one daughter, Susanna,
married to William Draper, Esq.;
of Adscomb in this
county, survived him; ye
two others dying in the
flower of their age, and
all ye sons very young,
except one nam'd John, who
deceased y{e} 24th March, 169$\frac{4}{5}$,
in ye 45th year of his age,
leaving one son, John, and
one daughter, Elizabeth.

The inscriptions on the other tablets abound with many curious specimens of antient orthography. Some of them are versified in Latin, and are highly interesting as classical productions. Beneath the tablet to the memory of George Evelyn, esq. who died in 1603, are carved his twenty-four children.

The church, including the chancel, is small, and contains but few ostensive memorials besides those already mentioned. The accommodations for the congregation are strong benches, placed in regular lines, and a few good pews for the principal families who attend. Above is a commodious gallery for singers; but, owing to the want of regular psalmody, it is but little used by that class.

The church-yard contains several neat monuments. All of them bear suitable inscriptions, whose names and dates serve to prove that the great arbiter has studied no distinction in his victims. Some of them are partially hidden by the unchecked luxuriance of the grass, and the epitaphs are scarcely perceptible for the thick dankish moss encrusted on their sides. One, however, appears to be of more recent date, consisting of a large slab of black marble, supported by two bronzed griffins, to the memory of Peter Campbell, esq., an opulent gentleman, formerly of the island of Jamaica, who retired to a beautiful villa in the adjoining parish, where he passed the evening of his life in perfect tranquillity. Behind the church I noticed a neat pedestal, supporting an urn to the memory of Mr. William Glanvill, one of the clerks of the treasury, and receiver of the revenues of the First Fruits office. Mr. G. was an eccentric benefactor to this and other parishes. He died in January, 171$\frac{7}{8}$, and by his will ordered, that, on the anniversary day of his death, forty shillings each should be paid to five poor boys of Wotton, upon condition that they shall, with their hands laid on his tomb, respectively repeat the Lord's Prayer, the Apostles' Creed, the Commandments, and part of the 15th chapter of Corinthians; and write, in a legible hand, two verses of the said chapter. The surplus of an annual bequest of £30, he ordered to be applied to other charitable purposes.

A broad walk, darkened by the thick foliage of two rows of trees, leads to the modernized porch; while another approach is by a rude flight of steps up the side of the hill. The whole cemetery bears an air of pensive solemnity, and seems well calculated to revive, in meditative melancholy, the sad recollection of the many scenes which have been witnessed within its walls. The fertilizing soil, likewise, tends to nourish crops of rank and flourishing weeds, which have, in some instances, completely overgrown the several little knolls.

The village rite of decorating and planting the graves of the defunct with flowers and evergreens, appears to be here entirely abolished, although, according to various authorities, this ceremony was universally prevalent at no very distant period. The origin of the custom may be traced to the Greeks and Romans, who considered it of such importance, as to have it expressed in their wills, in which they often directed roses to be strewed and planted on their graves, as specified by an old inscription at Ravenna, and another at Milan. Hence, Propertius has this expression;

" ———— et tenerâ poneret ossa Rosâ."

"We adorn their graves," says Evelyn, in his *Sylva*, " with flowers and redolent plants, just emblems of the life of man, which has been compared in Holy Scriptures to those fading beauties, whose roots, being buried in dishonour, rise again in glory." The rose, however, appears to have been the favoured flower among the antients; and of which Evelyn says, "this sweet flower, borne on a branch set with thorns, and accompanied with the lily, are natural hieroglyphics of our fugitive, umbratile, anxious, and transitory life, which, making so fair a show for time, is not yet without thorns and crosses." He also tells us that the custom was not altogether extinct in his time, near his dwelling in Surrey, "where the maidens yearly planted and decked the graves of their defunct sweethearts with rose-bushes." Camden, in his Britannia, remarks, "here also is a certain custom, observed time out of mind, of planting rose-trees upon the graves, especially by the young men and maidens, who have lost their loves: so that the church-yard is now full of them." This last-mentioned passage may, probably, allude to the church-yard at Ockley, a short distance from Wotton, of which Aubrey observes, "In the church-yard are many red rose-trees, planted among the graves, which have been there beyond man's memory. The sweetheart, (male or female) plants roses at the head of the grave of the lover deceased; a maid that lost her dear twenty years since, yearly hath the grave new turfed; and continues yet unmarried."

The unsophisticated feeling of sorrow which dictates these observances will be found abundantly scattered throughout the productions of our early poets. Thus Shakespeare's Arvigarus in Cymbeline:

——————— With fairest flowers,
Whilst summer lasts, and I live here, Fidele,
I'll sweeten thy sad grave:———————.
*   *   *   *   *
Yea, and furr'd moss, besides, when flowers are none,
To winter-ground thy corse.

ROUND DORKING. 141

The Hainanese have, also, to this day, a custom of visiting the tombs of their parents once a-year, in order to pluck away the weeds and grass from their graves, and freshen, with paints of different colours, the characters of their epitaphs: this they consider an imperious duty, and accordingly perform the ceremony with much solemnity.

The fastidiousness of artificial refinement has in most instances deposed these pleasing tributes of sincerity; and has filled our church-yards with objects by no means so well calculated to inspire the genuineness of emotion which we might feel in performing the last exequies at the grave of a friend, by decorating it with chaplets of flowers, or planting it with doleful evergreens.* Etiquette has thus

---

* "This usage," says the elegant author of the *Sketch Book*, " may still be met with in the church-yards of retired villages among the Welsh mountains: and I recollect an instance of it at the small town of Ruthen, which

contrived to declaim against this rite, and to substitute a series of pageant forms and ceremonies, which, however, are far exceeded in pathos and expression by the mournful minstrelsy and untutored sympathies of village funerals.

Wotton, or Wodeton, formerly gave name to this hundred. Mr. Aubrey supposes this to be the manor of Wodinton, mentioned in the charter of 30 Edward I. 1302, as then in the possession of William de Latimer, to whom a grant was

---

lies at the head of the beautiful vale of Clewyd. I have been told also," continues he, " by a friend, who was present at the funeral of a young girl in Glamorganshire, that the female attendants had their aprons full of flowers, which, as soon as the body was interred, they stuck about the grave. He noticed several graves which had been decorated in the same manner. As the flowers had been merely stuck in the ground, and not planted, they had soon withered, and might be seen in various states of decay; some drooping, others quite perished. They were afterwards to be supplanted by holly, rosemary, and other evergreens: which on some graves had grown to great luxuriance, and overshadowed the tombstones."

then made of two fairs to be held there. William, his second son, afterwards possessed the manor, then called Wodeton, which, upon his death in 1327, he left to his son. The parish is nine or ten miles from north to south; and near its extremity, on the borders of Sussex, is *Oakwood* chapel, a building apparently of considerable antiquity.

Adjoining Wotton, on the west, is *Abinger*, which, as Aubrey conjectures, received its name from Abin, an eminence or rising ground, the upper part of this parish being the most elevated spot in the county. The manor has been in the possession of the Evelyn family upwards of two centuries. The church, also, stands on very high ground. At the west end is a low wooden tower, rising from the roof, and surmounted with a low pyramidical spire, which presents a pleasing object in the landscape, viewed from the gate of Wotton church-yard.

In the parish of Abinger, on the road

to Leith-Hill, is *Parkhurst*. The residence, a neat structure, adjoins an extensive wood; and on the south, are some beautiful enclosures, containing about forty acres. The house has been for some time untenanted; notwithstanding, the estate forms an eligible retreat for the lover of rural retirement. The cottages on the road-side, and the neighbouring common, furnish many interesting scenes of humble life; and the native simplicity and inoffensive manners of their inhabitants well bespeak the true characteristics of the English peasant. Every thing in this spot bears the tranquil serenity of the sequestered village: the moss-clad cottage, the pleasant little green, the flower-garden, the wicket, the neatly-mended paling, and the green lanes, winding past the boundary of the adjoining estate—are objects which contribute to make up the most captivating features of an English landscape, whose harmony has not been disturbed by the sophistry of art. *Abinger-Hall*, a handsome and commodious villa, is situated on the north side of the Guildford road. This retired spot is now in the possession of James Scarlett, esq. M. P. whose profundity and eloquence as a lawyer and statesman are already well known. The house is delightfully placed on an eminence, surrounded by a fine lawn, plantations, and shrubbery; and the river, with a cascade in front. The contiguous scenery consists of woody knolls and bold rising hills, presenting rich successions of fascinating and picturesque country.

From Wotton church-yard gate, is the road to Leith-Hill, turning off through the venerable woods of Wotton-place, over Abinger-common, by Parkhurst, as above described.

A neat park-gate on the left of the road leads by the carriage-drive to *Wotton-Place*, environed with all its sylvan boast; and the prospect terminated by the bold outline of Leith-Hill, surmounted with its tower. The mansion is situate in the angle of two beautiful valleys, and near the junction of two streams, which are well supplied with water from the springs issuing out of the hill, to the south. It is celebrated as having been the residence of the Evelyns, since the reign of Queen Elizabeth; but more especially as the birth-place and retirement of JOHN EVELYN, esq., of whom the following biographical notice may not prove altogether incurious.

Descended from an antient, honourable, and opulent, house; established in a part of England, where he could partake of the delights of a country life, which no man loved more dearly, and the advantages of science and society, which no man could estimate more justly, or more entirely enjoy,—the life of JOHN EVELYN may be regarded as one of the most admirable portraits of the genuine English character. Trained up in the geniality of a generous and constitutional spirit of loyalty, and in the true principles of the church establishment, he was neither swayed by the rancour and bitterness of political or puritanical party-spirit.

Such a character is in itself amiable and estimable; and, in these untoward times, a visit to the site where the true philosopher once indulged in all the various pursuits of literature and science, cannot fail to prove interesting to the reflective mind. The birth-place—the nursery— the school—the residence—and the death-place of this admirable man, are alike consecrated by the purity of so perfect a model of moral worth and excellence. Every object connected with those seasons becomes enhanced in our minds, by communicating with a chain of associations, which animate the contemplatist with recollections of his greatness; and lead him into a train of musings, copiously stored with *materiel*.

Such were my feelings as I approached that venerable pile of building—Wotton House, where John Evelyn was born in October, 1620. Richard Evelyn, his father, possessed an estate of about £4,000 a-year, "well-wooded and full of timber."* At four years old, he was taught to read by the village schoolmaster, over the porch of Wotton church; and, at six, his picture, (to use his own words,) " was drawn in oyl, by Chatterell, no ill painter.†"

---

* "To give an instance of what store of woods and timber of prodigious size there were grown in our little county of Surrey, my own grandfather had standing at Wotton, and about that estate, timber that now were worth 100,000*l.* Since of what was left my father, (who was a great preserver of wood,) there has been 30,000*l.* worth of timber fallen by the axe, and the fury of the hurricane (in 1703, by which upwards of 1000 trees were blown down;)—now no more, Wotton stript and naked, and ashamed almost to own its name."

Sylva, book III. chap. 7.

† This picture, if still in possession of the family, would form an invaluable treasure in the cabinet of the virtuoso; and would, doubtless, give rise to some curious conjectures among the physiognomists of the present day.

After studying some time at Lewes and Eton, in 1636 he entered the Temple, and, in the following year, he was placed as a fellow-commoner at Baliol college, Oxford. During the last year of his residence there, his younger brother came to be his chamber fellow. Both soon removed to the Middle Temple: and, about three months after this, their father died.*

The signs of the times were now too evident to be mistaken. Outrages had been committed in various parts, and libels and invectives were actively sowing the seeds of dissention in all directions. Evelyn had been present at the trial of the Earl of Strafford, and had witnessed " the fatal stroke which severed from its

---

* In his *Diary*, is the following passage:—" 1641, 2d January. We at night followed the mourning hearse to the church at Wotton, where after a sermon and funeral oration my father was interred near his formerly erected monument, and mingled with the ashes of our mother, his deare wife."

shoulders, the wisest head in England." In this portentous state of affairs, he resolved on quitting this country for the continent. He remained about three months in the Netherlands, and then returned home. Soon after this, the civil war broke out, and Evelyn went with his horse and arms to join the king. He did not remain there long, but retired to his brother's house at Wotton, where he began to improve the gardens.

When the covenant was pressed, Evelyn absented himself, and, having obtained the king's license to travel, he set out, accompanied by an old fellow-collegian, named Thicknesse. He passed through France, into Italy, after having witnessed the chief objects of popular curiosity; and, having remained in Italy two years, he met with a Mr. Abdy, a man of much modesty and erudition; Waller, the poet; and one Captain Wray;—in whose company he set out on his return. Having reached Paris, Evelyn resolved to sojourn in that city, where he learnt the German and Spanish tongues, and frequented a course of chemistry; and having become intimate in the family of Sir Richard Browne, the British resident ambassador at the court of France, he married his daughter, then in her fourteenth year, he being twenty-seven. About three months after his marriage, he was called into England, leaving his wife with her parents. Charles was at that time in the hands of his enemies. Evelyn remained in England until after "unkingship" had been proclaimed, when he obtained a passport for France.

Evelyn returned to England in 1650, and, notwithstanding his warm attachment to the royalists, he remained for some time unmolested. Sayes Court, the estate of his father-in-law, at Deptford, was at this time suffering from want of being secured from the usurpers. He was advised to reside on it, and compound with the government, which Charles authorized him to do: and, at the same time, charged him with the perilous commission of corresponding with him and his ministers.

The estate at Deptford, when it became Evelyn's property, consisted of pasture-land, an orchard, and a holly hedge.* This afforded fine scope for the exercise of the philosopher's ingenious mind, and was, afterwards, the fruit of those efforts, in which he developed his great capabilities for ornamental gardening, a branch of science which hitherto had never flourished in England.

At the time Evelyn commenced his

---

* When the Czar of Muscovy came to England in 1698, he was desirous of having the use of Sayes Court, as being near the King's Dock-Yard, at Deptford, where that monarch proposed instructing himself in the art of ship-building. During his stay, he did so much damage, that Mr. Evelyn had an allowance of 150*l.* for it. One of the Czar's favourite recreations was being wheeled in a barrow through the holly-hedge, which provoked the philosopher to make the following observation: "*Thanks to the Czar for spoiling my garden.*"

horticultural labours, there were no examples for imitation. All was devised by his own active mind, and consequently guided by the taste of his age. This subject did not, however, wholly engross his attention: and, although not an actual proselyte to the doctrine of vegetable diet, his industry in the culture of plants and obtaining a knowledge of their several properties was unremitted.

Evelyn was staunchly opposed to the arch villany and tyrannical abuses of Cromwell's government. Fanaticism, and the wildest extravagances of political feuds then agitated and convulsed the country, until the atrocities of the usurper brought on a premature decay, embittering his latter days with the stinging consciousness of his crimes. The death of the Protector was far from allaying the angry spirit which his conduct had stirred up. His brother was treated with indignity; "parties and pretenders strove for the government; and all was anarchy and confusion." Evelyn had hitherto been little more than a bye-stander in this political storm: his garden and plantations had in the mean time become the subjects of popular conversation; and, in the course of his retirement, he had published some useful and important works. These were, " a translation of the first book of Lucretius:" " St. Chrysostom's Golden Book for the education of Children;" and " the French Gardener and English Vineyard."

At the commencement of the restoration, Evelyn came forward, and notwithstanding the danger attendant on the enterprize, he published an apology for the royal party and the king. Besides the satisfaction of having rendered his country a most essential service, Evelyn had private reasons for rejoicing in the restoration of Charles II. It brought home his father-in-law, Sir Richard Browne, after nineteen years' exile; and thus largely contributed to his domestic happiness.

He was constantly received at court by Charles, with his usual affability, and was on terms of close intimacy with the king, who nominated him one of the council of the Royal Society. He was soon after chosen one of the commissioners for correcting various mal-practices in the city of London; and in 1664, when war was declared against the Dutch, he was appointed one of the commissioners for taking care of the sick and wounded prisoners. The duty was grievously onerous; and, in the midst of this distress, the plague broke out in London, and swept off from 4 to 5000 persons weekly. The contagion soon spread: Evelyn sent his wife and family to Wotton, but staid himself to look after his charges. The ravages of the pestilence did not however dismay him in the fulfilment of his duty; he resisted them with the zeal and humanity of a true philanthropist, for which he afterwards received the personal thanks of the king.

On Sept. 2, 1666, the ever-memorable fire broke out in London, and spread fresh calamities and devastation in that quarter. Evelyn was an eye-witness of that destructive conflagration, and remarked that he never observed such general resignation or less repining among sufferers: the disaster gave but few obstacles to the regular channel of mercantile affairs; and the ruins had scarcely ceased smoking, when Charles actually introduced a new fashion of dress, formed upon the Persian mode. Our philosopher, at this time, beheld with heartfelt regret, the profligacy of the court, and the defective state of the national morals. Gaming, brutal sports, and the degenerating licentiousness of the stage, had corrupted many of his contemporaries; and, in the midst of these immoralities, his life presented an uniform example of public and private virtues; and, racked as was that age by civil and religious factions, Evelyn had no enemy.

In 1694, he left Sayes Court, to pass the remainder of his days at Wotton. About five years after, his brother died. The remainder of his life was spent in that unembittered repose, which those, whose past life has been so honourably spent, can only enjoy. The reproaches of conscience never intruded on the serenity of his private hours; his manners and disposition ensured him universal respect; and in this happy old age, he fell asleep, in the year 1706.

The summary of his public deeds will remain in the pages of our history, as everlasting memorials of true patriotism, benevolence, and unerring rectitude of conduct. Whether in the closet, or the wide field of public action, he cherished that friendship and esteem, which attended him to his grave, and has immortalized his name in the memory of succeeding ages. Nothing which innovation can adduce will impair his celebrity. As an author, his talents, though not prominent, were applied to subjects of practical utility. His *Sylva* becomes a work of national importance, from its valuable information on the methods by which Britain has triumphantly maintained the superiority in her naval strength. His Diary, or Kalendarium may be considered as one of the most finished specimens of autobiography in the whole compass of English literature—presenting a true PICTURE OF HIS TIMES, sketched with rare fidelity, neither winking at the follies and vices of Royalty, nor sullying his pages with the acrimony of their unprofitable contentions. Although an intimate friend of Charles II. and James II., he utterly discountenanced their arbitrary measures. His mind, unbigoted by sects, granted universal toleration in its most extended latitude. His diligence in the discharge of public duties ranked him as a faithful servant, both to his sovereign and to his country. When retired from the busy hum of public life, the hours of his solitude were advantageously filled up with promoting the interests of his fellow creatures, and in recording the events of his life, the details of which have already afforded many hours of pure delight to the curious and historical reader. His Memoirs, together with a selection of familiar letters and private correspondence, were published in 1818, in two handsome quarto volumes; and both in point of editorial arrangement and typographical elegance, they may be considered as a valuable acquisition to the library of the man of letters. The original MSS. and documents descended with the estate to the late Sir Frederick Evelyn, bart. This gentleman, dying without issue, entrusted the whole to the late Lady Evelyn, by whom they were delivered to W. Bray, esq. a gentleman of considerable antiquarian research, and under whose able superintendence the work was printed,*the last sheets of which,

---

* Mr. Bray has long resided at the village of *Sheire*, a short distance from Wotton; and, although upwards of

with a dedication to Lady E. were actually in the hands of the printer at the hour of her death.

Among the honourable events of Mr. Evelyn's life, it should not be forgotten, that, as the first treasurer of Greenwich Hospital, he laid the foundation-stone of that splendid establishment. In 1662, when the Royal Society was established, he was appointed one of the first Fellows in Council, and took an active part in its establishment and conduct. He procured Mr. Howard's library to be given to them; and, in 1667, the Arundelian Marbles to the university of Oxford. Among his numerous plans, he proposed to Mr. Boyle, in 1659, to found a philo-

---

fourscore, his exertions are still as arduous as ever in the cause of literature and science. The veteran services of this gentleman well qualified him for such a task, and in the execution of it, he has by no means disappointed the expectations of our *literati*, among whom great anxiety had been manifested for the publication of these valuable and important documents.

sophical college for retirement; and, the country being at that time distracted by court intrigues and popular fury, he is said to have commenced a model of this scheme at his brother's seat at Wotton.

He was the last sheriff of the counties of Surrey and Sussex jointly; on which occasion he attended the judges with 116 servants in green satin doublets and cloth cloaks, guarded with silver galloon, as were the brims of their hats, which were adorned with white feathers. These men carried new javelins; and two trumpeters bore banners, on which were emblazoned his arms. There were, besides, thirty gentlemen, to whom he was uncle, or great uncle, all clad in the same colours, who came with several others to do him honour.

Mr. Horace Walpole, in the course of the many elegant and faithful pictures of men and manners, which he has so admirably drawn in his *Catalogue of Engra-*

vers, gives the following sketch of the character of Mr. Evelyn:*

"I mean not to write his life," says this intelligent author, "but I must observe that his life was a course of enquiry, study, curiosity, instruction, and benevolence. The works of the Creator, and the minute labours of the creature, were all objects of his pursuit. He unfolded the perfection of the one, and assisted the imperfection of the other. He adored from examination; was a courtier that flattered only by informing his prince, and by pointing out what was worthy for him to countenance."

A single retrospect of the life of this celebrated philosopher, and the times in which he flourished, teems with interesting incident, and introduces us to one of the most important epochs of English history. He lived in the busy reigns of Charles I., Cromwell, Charles II., James II., and William III.; although a court

---

* Mr. Evelyn was an engraver, and published some views between Rome and Naples, drawn by him in his travels.

favourite of two of those monarchs, no ambition for royal or popular distinction or applause ever induced him to swerve from a conscientious and unbiassed discharge of his public duties. He was, also, in habits of close intimacy with the most eminent men of those days: foreigners distinguished for learning or the arts, who came to England, seldom left it without visiting him; and the prudent course which he took in the political affairs of his time, proves him to have been actuated only by a spirit of genuine and disinterested patriotism. His literary contemporaries consisted of some of the brightest luminaries which this country has produced; among whom we may recognize the venerated names of MILTON, COWLEY, MARVELL, DRYDEN, LOCKE, NEWTON, SWIFT, SHAFTESBURY, ADDISON, BOLINGBROKE, POPE, and GAY. We may, indeed, challenge history to produce so many men of splendid genius living within an equal period of time; and when it is considered how congenial their society must have been to the taste and disposition of Evelyn, he must be considered as having been equally well suited to the age in which he lived.

I was now induced to make some attempt to gain admittance to view the interior of the library. The house, although in a valley, is actually on part of Leith-Hill, the rise from thence being very gradual. Evelyn describes it in his *Diary*, as "large and antient, suitable to those hospitable times, and so sweetly environed with those delicious streams and venerable woods, as in the judgment of strangers as well as Englishmen, it may be compared to one of the most pleasant Seates in the nation, most tempting to a great person and a wanton purse to render it conspicuous: it has rising grounds, meadows, woods, and water, in abundance." His Diary likewise contains a fac-simile of a curious autographic sketch of Wotton House in 1653, in which the grounds appear laid out according to the fantastical custom of that period. Much of the antient house yet remains. The library, on the north side, was built by the philosopher's son, Sir John Evelyn, who was created a baronet in 1713. He inherited the literary taste, as well as the patrimony, of his ancestors, and lived here universally beloved and respected. The drawing-room in the south front was added by Sir Frederic.* The whole is a quaint and irregular pile of building, and exhibits the various additions and improvements made by its respective proprietors.

My guide, a female servant, led me to the library, which opens by a glazed door on a fine sheet of lawn. The dimensions are 45 feet in height, 14 width, and as many length. The curious collection of books was considerably augmented by the late

---

* Sir F. Evelyn was much attached to the sports of the turf and the chase. He maintained the establishment at Wotton with the same spirit of hospitality, for which his family had been so long distinguished; and died in 1812.

Lady Evelyn, who likewise had a complete catalogue arranged by Mr. Upcott, of the London Institution. In addition to the printed works, there are several valuable papers on every subject, written by the celebrated philosopher, whose indefatigable industry was such, that in his extensive and voluminous correspondence during his long life, he never employed an amanuensis : he has also left transcripts, in his own hand, of great numbers of letters, both received and sent ; and, among his MSS. is a bible, bound in three volumes, the pages filled with notes.

I amused myself with looking cursorily over the shelves, and found several works which would prove highly gratifying to the bibliographer, and were worthy of a more deliberate examination. Near the chimney-piece I noticed several bound pamphlets, among which were "An Apology for the Royal Party," and " The late News, or Message from Brussels unmasked;" both of which were published by John Evelyn in 1659. They present a curious specimen of the typographic art at that time, and, in their literary character, they may perhaps be said to resemble the most popular political *jeux d'esprits* of the present day.

I reluctantly left this bibliographical treasury, and, enquiring for the portrait of the philosopher, by Sir Godfrey Kneller, the girl replied "M'ap you mean *Sylvy* Evelyn, sir;" and, accordingly, led me to the drawing-room, where I found the original in excellent preservation, surrounded by several other paintings. An old table of a solid piece of beech, about six feet in diameter, is shewn as one of the curiosities of the house.*

My guide now led me to the grounds on the south side of the house. Here I found a basin of water, with a fountain in

---

* The *philosopher's table*, mentioned in his *Sylva*, formed of a large *oak* plank, is now destroyed.

the centre, and a temple, containing some allegorical figures supplied with water, which they disgorge into small basins beneath. The temple, or colonnade, is backed by full-grown firs, on the other side of which is a beautiful lawny track, communicating with the noble beech woods by several winding walks, which not only present a delightful retreat for the contemplatist, but, at the same time, inspire him with many grateful reminiscences of their former possessors. Adjoining the pleasure-grounds, is a large enclosed flower-garden, which was to have formed one of the principal objects in the philosopher's "Elysium Britannicum." This idea has been partly realized by the late Lady Evelyn, who arranged the flower-garden and green-house, which she also embellished with several curious plants and flowers, both native and exotic. The latter adjoins the mansion, and my guide informed me, that, previous to the last illness, her ladyship passed much time in her green-house, in the arrangement of which, her taste for botany was happily displayed. She died in London, in 1817, aged seventy-two, after a lingering illness, which had long baffled all medical skill.

Her ladyship was the only daughter of William Turton, esq. of Staffordshire. As the relict and descendant of the pious and learned John Evelyn, she took pride in preserving the memorials of that antient and honourable family, of which she considered herself the representative. Like her venerable predecessor, she lived not for herself: those who were favoured with her friendship will cheerfully bear testimony to the urbanity of her manners and general kindness. Her death was, also, deeply deplored by the numerous poor in her neighbourhood, to whom she proved a constant benefactress. By her will, she returned this estate to her family, devising it to John Evelyn, esq., who descended from George Evelyn, esq. the purchaser of the same in 1579.

Bordering on the woods, is a broad gravelled walk, which, in the life-time of Lady Evelyn, was constantly swept clean by several aged women, who subsisted on her weekly bounty. The rivulet winding through the valley is diversified with several little falls, and was formerly of great importance. Mr. Evelyn, in a letter to Mr. Aubrey, dated 8th February, 1675, says "that on the stream near his house formerly stood many powder-mills, erected by his ancestors, who were the very first that brought that invention into England; before which we had all our powder from Flanders."* He also says, "that on this stream were set up the first brass mills for casting, hammering into plates, and

---

* He gives an account of one of these mills blowing up, which broke a beam, 15 inches in diameter, at Wotton-Place; and states that one standing lower down towards Sheire, on blowing up, shot a piece of timber through a cottage, which took off a poor woman's head, as she was spinning.

cutting and drawing into wire, that were in England: also, a fulling mill, and a mill for hammering iron, all of which are now demolished. Such a variety of mills on so narrow a brook, and so little a compass at that time, was not to be met with in any other part of England." The last of these mills gave name to a small street or hamlet in the parish of Abinger, which, to this day, is called the HAMMER. Another stream, taking its rise at the base of Leith-Hill, winds its way to Dorking, where it takes the name of Pipbrook, and, supplying six corn mills, in the course of two miles, finally empties itself into the river Mole, under Box-hill.

The Rookery, adjoining the Wotton estate, is situate on the bank of the last of these streams. It was some time the property of Abraham Tucker, esq., of Betchworth Castle, of whom it was purchased in 1759, by Daniel Malthus, esq.,*

---

* Mr. Malthus died at *Albury*, near Guildford, in Jan. 1800. He was the admired, though for some time un-

father of the celebrated political œconomist of that name. The residence was formerly an obscure farm-house, called Chert-gate.

Mr. Malthus first took advantage of the beauties of hill and dale, wood and water, in this estate, and converted it into an elegant seat, to which he gave the present appellation. In 1768, he sold it to Richard Fuller, esq., by whom it was considerably enlarged, and left at his death, in 1782, to his son. By him it was devised to Richard Fuller, esq., the present proprietor. The residence is situated about a quarter of a mile south of the main road, in a narrow vale, enclosed with hanging hills. The whole of the building is rough-cast, surmounted with battle-

---

known, translator of the Sorrows of Werter; of an Essay on Landscape, from the French of the Marquis D'Ermenonville, and of the elegant translation of Paul et Virginia, published by Mr. Dodsley, under the title of Paul and Mary. His works evince that Mr. Malthus was a man of taste and learning, and among his friends he was esteemed for his modesty, liberality, and many amiable qualities. He is buried in Wotton church-yard.

mented parapets and gothic pinnacles. The descent from the front is by a beautiful sloping lawn to the margin of a fine pool of water, in the centre of which is a small island, overgrown with shrubs and exotics. The hill behind the house is clothed with a fine beech wood, extending a considerable distance, and intersected by serpentine walks, which formerly led to several romantic buildings, with appropriate dedications.

The foot-path (a public thoroughfare,) passes the front of the tasteful residence. A bye-path branches off to the left, and winds on the brink of an extensive sheet of water. The imagination can scarcely conceive a scene, of the kind, more complete than this. In the centre is a small island, on which is a ruinous fishing house, partially hidden by trees and evergreens; while, from this group, rise two or three tall firs, which give an air of wildness and romantic beauty to the whole expanse, shaded on all sides with trees and shrubs to the water's edge, and winding out of sight.

A narrow strip of green lawn bordering the water, and spreading at length into a small meadow, forms all the rest of the grounds which is not occupied with wood. Plantations of beeches and other tall timber trees, fill the remaining space, insulating (as it were) the whole with a belt of forest scenery, and securing to it a character of coolness and sequestered retreat. The hottest and most sunny season of the year seems the time for enjoying this place to full advantage. In dark and chilly weather, it must, probably, appear to superabound with shade and moisture; yet the site of the house is tolerably cheerful and open. A boat-house, a rude ice-house, and a small corn-mill, complete this enchanting spot, unparalleled in rusticity and picturesque effect.

The scenery of this estate is, altogether, of the finest order. Water, which constitutes one of its principal features, runs throughout the grounds, in some places having the appearance of a glassy lake, and, in others, that of a bubbling stream. The borders consist of successions of cragged precipices, and retired glens, shaded by stately foliage, and abounding with delightful nooks.

The main path passes a rustic temple, over the door of which appears the following quotation from Virgil:

" ⸺Pan curat oves, oviumque magistros,"

The front is closed in by a grotesque fence, formed of the limbs of trees, nailed together. The back of this curious edifice proves to be a *cow-house!* and forms a warm shelter for cattle. The pediment is supported by columns covered with bark, so as to resemble the trunks of trees; and the sides are formed of laths filled in with moss.

I lingered some time amidst these scenes of sylvan solitude, and at length quitted them by ascending a hilly field, from which I caught a glimpse of the mansion at Bury-hill, embosomed in all its rising woods and plantations.

A narrow and winding chalky road leads to another dell, in which is placed *Filbrook Lodge*, belonging to Robert Barclay, esq., the proprietor of Bury-hill. This estate was for some time the property of Daniel Franco Haynes, esq., who, in 1821, disposed of it to Mr. Barclay. The residence, a neat structure, is charmingly situated at an agreeable distance from the public thoroughfare; and the hills in the back ground, by filling up the scene, give a peculiarly fine effect to the whole. In the front of the house are two neat pedestals, supporting ornamental urns; and a small *jet d'eau* is constantly throwing forth a limpid stream, which, returning to its destined basin, breaks the silence that prevails all around. Contiguous to the road is a curious cascade, overhung with trees, the water falling nearly sixty feet from the supereminent rock, over the several graduated ledges or descents, into a small stone basin.

In the centre of the stream opposite, is a thatched fishing hut, built of stones, so as to resemble a rustic grotto, with an approach by a small wooden bridge; affording a cool retreat for the angler. The stream, which winds itself through the estate, is pleasingly varied with several small falls, which not only add to the elegance of the scene, but contribute to delight the ear, by their gentle murmurings.

The general character of this valley is gay and cheerful, notwithstanding its sequestered situation. The embellishments consist of two neat bridges crossing the stream, pedestals, urns, decorative pillars, statues, and other productions of the plastic mould, which appear here and there intermingled with shrubbery walks and banks, overgrown with hanging weeds. Such are the features which characterize these peaceful regions of retirement, which seem well fitted for "the exercise of those studies, by which we come at the knowledge of an infinity almost of things throughout all nature."

Among the natural curiosities of this neighbourhood, is *Mag's Well*, situate two miles south-east of Wotton-hatch, in the parish of Dorking, on a farm called *Meriden*, about three miles from the town. The following interesting information is the substance of a letter, on this subject, communicated by an intelligent gentleman of the neighbourhood, and addressed to the editors of the Gazette of Health.

"That Mag's Well, and the salutary power ascribed to its waters, are of great antiquity, cannot be doubted; inasmuch, as Cardon, Aubrey, and other authors, particularly describe the spring as possessing powerful medicinal qualities. In scrofulous and cutaneous disorders, whether of the human or canine species, it has, time out of mind, been deemed equally efficacious; there being, as I understand, not only a convenient place of bathing for bipeds, but a species of bath for quadrupeds, which are frequently brought from a distance, to be cured of various distempers by immersion in Mag's Well, which in summer, it is said, is colder, and in winter warmer, than the water of other springs.

"Taken internally, the water was long believed to be at once strongly cathartic and emetic. That opinion has probably been less prevalent since the publication of Manning's Surrey, in which, these alleged properties are strongly controverted, although, in that work, it is said to be detergent.

"Finding, however, that many of the country people continue to put great faith in the virtue of 'Mag's Wells,' I resolved personally to examine what is esteemed one of the curiosities of Surrey.

"The farm on which the well is situated belongs to the College, Guildford, and is in the tenantry of George Dewdney, esq., banker, remote from any public road, and embosomed in woods. A pedestrian excursion to the vale in which the spring rises, appeared the only mode by which I could obtain my object; the obscurity in which the well is hidden, rendering it inaccessible to a carriage, and almost to a horse, for nearly the last mile of approach.

"The bath, or well, is comprehended within a building, the sides and ends of which are joined into right angles; but there is no roof. Immediately opposite the entrance of the building is the door-way to the bath; into which there is a descent of five steps: the bath is in length about seven feet, and in width and in depth between four and five feet. The water enters at an aperture on the right, and the surplus, when the bath is full, discharges itself over a lip on the left; the whole can be readily run off through a vent at the bottom, and at the left-hand corner, by drawing a plug.—The whole structure has, apparently, been for some time much neglected. The entrance and the exit of the water being imperfect, the bath was nearly empty, the depth not being more than three or four inches.

"Although the day was extremely cold, there did not appear any extraordinary sensation of coldness on immersing the hand in the well; and the mercury of a thermometer, the bulb of which was immersed for ten minutes, did not descend much below fifty.

"A taste differing from ordinary spring-water was not positively to be discriminated; certainly, not the slightest perception of saline particles could be distinguished. The only taste I could fancy I detected was that of iron, but in so slight a degree, as to preclude all positive assertion of the fact. In order, however, to ascertain if the powers imputed to the water of the spring are, or are not, fallacious, a scientific examination of its properties would undoubtedly be satisfactory to the public: I have therefore directed a quantity of water to be taken from the well, and sent to you, sufficient, I conceive, for analysis, in the hope that you may not deem it unworthy of your notice.

Dorking, December, 1817.   J. M.

The water of Mag's Well, on accurate analysis, proves to be slightly impregnated with the sulphate of magnesia and iron. It is entirely free from calcareous matter, and approaches very nearly to the Malvern water. It may prove beneficial as an alterative, and in obviating costiveness; but, to produce an aperient effect, it must be combined with the sulphate of magnesia, or the sulphate of soda."*

A quantity of Anglo-Saxon coins were lately discovered on *Winterfield Farm*, in this neighbourhood; on which the following paper has been published by the Society of Antiquaries of London, in vol. xix. of the *Archæologia*.

---
* Gazette of Health, Jan. 1818.

An Account of some Anglo-Saxon Pennies, found at Dorking in Surrey. Communicated by Taylor Combe, *Esq. Secretary of the Royal Society.* 12*th March*, 1818.

A very interesting discovery of a considerable number of Anglo-Saxon pennies having been made last year in the neighbourhood of Dorking, I feel great pleasure in being able to communicate an account of them to the Society of Antiquaries. The field in which the coins were found belongs to the Rev. Mr. Turner, and was at that time, and is still, in the occupation of George Dewdney, esq. It is situated in the parish of Dorking, in Surrey, at a short distance from the Roman road called Stone-street, leading out of Sussex through Surrey to London; and near the camp called Hanstie-Bury, which is of a circular form, and has the banks of ditches nearly perfect at this time. Mr. Manning is inclined to consider this camp as Danish.

The coins were found in the month of April, 1817, by a ploughman, who was at work in the field. The plough struck against something, which, on examination, proved to be a wooden box, containing about seven hundred Saxon coins, and about six ounces of fragments of coins. The wood, of which the box was made, crumbled to pieces immediately, so that it was not possible to ascertain either its form or dimensions. The coins, particularly those which lay uppermost, were cemented firmly together by metallic incrustations of a green and blue colour, which were carbonates of copper formed by the decomposition of the metal used as an alloy to the silver. The coins were lying about ten or twelve inches below the surface of the ground, in a spot where the colour of the earth is particularly black, and which has always been remarked to produce better corn than any other part of the field.

The following is a list of the kings whose coins were contained in this parcel, together with the number of coins belonging to each king.

Kings of the West Saxons.		Arbp. of Canterbury.	
Æthelweard	16	Ceolnoth	86
Kings of Mercia.		**Sole Monarchs.**	
Ciolvulf I.	1	Eegbeorht	20
Biornwulf	1	Ethelvulf	263
Wiglaf	1	Æthelbearht	249
Berhtulf	23	**King of Soissons.**	
Burgred	1	Pipin	1
Kings of the East Angles.			
Eadmund	3		
Ethelstan	3		

These coins, with about 40 others which I have not seen, and which were dispersed soon after they were found, constituted the whole number.

[Here is introduced a description of the several coins belonging to each prince, with references to authors who have written on them; particularly to the Rev. Rogers Ruding, whose work has lately appeared.]

Æthelheard [so in the *Archæologia*, and not Æthelweard as in preceding list], king of the West Saxons, began his reign in 726, and it was not before the year 855 that Eadmund was king of the East Angles. There is in fact no king of the name of Æthelweard among the kings of the West Saxons; and it seems probable that the English antiquarians, not finding the name of Æthelweard in the list of Saxon kings, were led to appropriate the coins with this name to Æthelheard, a king of the West Saxons, whose name resembles that of Æthelweard more than any other, both in sound and orthography.

[In this manner the coins are explained, always referring to Ruding's work and copying the inscriptions from it. The last coin is that of Pipin king of Soissons in the North of France, on which is this remark.—"This coin, belonging to the father of Charlemagne, is the only foreign coin that was found in the parcel."]

From the time when the princes reigned whose coins have been found, they could not have been buried in the earth before 870, in which year Ethelstan began his reign. And it could not have been long after that time, as no coins are found of any successor of Ceolnoth in the see of Canterbury, (who sat from 830 to 870,) or of the successors of Æthelbaerth among the sole monarchs, and he reigned from 860 to 866.

I have now nothing more to add, except to state the means by which I have been enabled to examine so large a portion of the coins discovered at Dorking: and, in doing this, I feel infinite pleasure in acknowledging the great obligations the British Museum is under to ROBERT BARCLAY, esq. of *Bury-hill* in the county of Surrey, who, fortunately for the cause of science, became the proprietor of 553 of these coins, which he purchased on the spot. This gentleman, with a liberality entitled to the highest praise, immediately sent the whole of his collection to me, requesting that I would select for the British Museum every coin not already in the National collection. The Museum is also under obligations to GEORGE DEWDNEY, esq. of Dorking, in Surrey, who sent, for my inspection, 100 coins found in the same parcel, and handsomely allowed me to retain, for the Trustees of the British Museum, several pieces not already in their collection. The Museum has, by these means, received the important addition of 174 coins, in the Anglo-Saxon series; and with the exception of three coins, namely Ciolvulf I., Beornvulf, and Wiglaf, it now possesses a specimen of every coin recorded in the present account.

March 12, 1818.

The printed account occupies pages 109-119; *and the plates (No. 9 and 10 of the volume,) contain, in all, 26 coins, both obverse and reverse.*

The upper end of the Fillbrook estate terminates in a wild track or valley, called *Broadmoor*, which contains a few small cottages, occupied by labouring poor. The sides of the hills were overgrown with brakes, interspersed with heath in bloom; and on their summits appeared a few straggling cottages, with an ascent by a flight of steps, formed out of the bank.

Reaching the end of the valley, the retrospective scenery of Broadmoor has a pleasing effect, and presents a truly picturesque glen. The road now winds over a black naked moor, rising into the celebrated LEITH-HILL. The ascent on this side is very gentle; and the elevation would scarcely be suspected, were it not for the glorious prospect that bursts on the sight at the further extremity. Any detail that can be given of this enchanting scene must, however, fall short of the following description, written by JOHN DENNIS, in a letter to his friend, Mr. Serjeant.*

* See his Letters, familiar, moral, and critical, vol. i.

"In a late journey I took through Surrey, (says Mr. D.) I passed over a hill, which showed me a more transporting sight than ever the country had shown me before, either in England or Italy. The prospects which in Italy pleased me the most, were, the Valdarno from the Appennines; Rome and the Mediterranean from the mountains of Viterbo, the former at forty and the latter at fifty miles distance; and the Campagna of Rome from Tivoli and Frescati: from which places you see every foot of that famous Champagne, even from the bottom of the Tivoli and Frescati to the very foot of the mountains of Viterbo, without any thing to intercept your sight. But from a hill I passed in my late journey, I had a prospect more extensive than any of these, and which surpassed them at once in rural charms, pomp, and magnificence—the hill which I speak of is called LEITH-HILL, and is situated about six miles south of Dorking. It juts out about two miles beyond that range of hills which terminates the north Downs on the south. When I saw from one of those hills, at about two miles distance, that side of Leith-Hill which faces the Downs, it appeared the most beautiful prospect I had ever seen. But, after we had conquered the hill itself, I saw a sight that would transport a stoic; a sight that looked like enchantment and a vision beatific! Beneath us lay open to our view all the wilds of Surrey and Sussex, and a great part of those of Kent, admirably diversified in every part of them with woods, and fields of corn and pasture, and every where adorned with stately rows of trees."

"This beautiful vale is about thirty miles in breadth, and about sixty in length, and is terminated to the south by the majestic range of the southern hills and the sea; and it is no easy matter to decide, whether the hills, which appear thirty, forty, or fifty miles distance, with their tops in the sky, seem more awful and venerable, or the delicious vale between you and them more inviting. About noon, on a serene day, you may, at thirty miles distance, see the water of the sea through a chasm of the mountain; (that is of the South Downs, called Becting Gap;) and that, above all, which makes it a noble and wonderful prospect is, that, at the very time when, at thirty miles distance, you behold the very water of the sea, at the same time you behold to the southward the most delicious rural prospect in the world. At the same time, by a little turn of your head towards the north, you look full over Box-Hill, and see the country beyond it between that and London; and, over the very stomachers of it, see St. Paul's, at twenty-five miles distance, and London beneath it, and Hampstead and Highgate beyond it!"

"These observations," says Mr. Bucke,*

---
* Philosophy of Nature, vol. ii.

"derive additional interest, when we consider the source whence they proceed;—a giant in learning,—a hornet in criticism, and an indignant observer of the dispensations of fortune."

No language can fully describe the thrilling ecstacy, on the first view of this magnificent scene. The eye, wearied with the barren and uninteresting aspect of the neighbouring hills, is suddenly relieved by a burst of panoramic beauty, unrivalled by the prospects from Snowdon, Cader Idris, and even all the boasted charms of Swiss scenery. No one ever ascended Leith-hill, but felt his soul elevated, and his whole frame invigorated, with beholding the richness and splendour of the expanse lying at his feet. Scenes like these have ever proved a fertile source of display for the philosopher, the poet, and the painter. Besides furnishing subject-matter for reflection and reverie, they possess sites, full of vigour and interest, which communicate as by a secret-spring, with an endless train of classical and historical associations. Every town and hamlet has its favoured spot, consecrated either as the birth-place of some literary luminary, or storied in the legendary page, as the field where liberty wrested itself from the ruthless grasp of oppression, and bards first sung the triumphs of their native land. All these reminiscences give rise to soul-subduing reflections.

The periods of viewing, likewise, lend alternate charms to this prospect. The early mists dispelled by the gorgeous beams of the rising sun unfold to us the wide expanse, invigorated by the coolness and fragrance of the morning breeze. —At the decline of day, when the sun sinks behind the western hills, in all his dying splendour, the scene is truly magnificent:—when all is silent, except the unstudied melody of the shepherd's pipe stealing through the landscape, and serving to remind us of the happy idyls of pastoral life.—How delightful to wander o'er the valley, or trace it from the summit of this glorious eminence, until the soft shades of twilight gradually envelope its beauties.*

These, however, are but the general features of the prospect. The whole circumference is, at least, TWO HUNDRED MILES, which far exceeds that of the Keep and Terrace at Windsor Castle, over which you may see as far as the eye, un-

---

* On one occasion, I recollect visiting this spot, during a summer storm; the scene was truly interesting. The rain poured down in torrents, and, for a short time, all was lost in an ocean of mist. A calm succeeded—the sun shone forth with increased lustre—and presently the landscape re-appeared—the smiling verdure of the trees and fields seemed to be renovated by the fertilizing shower—the air was cool and serene—and all nature had acquired additional charms of fascinating loveliness. As I returned through the shady lanes of *Wotton* and *Westcott*, the delicious woodbine filled the air with its perfume, while the boughs were thickly hung with rain-drops, which glistened in the broad glare of sun-set, and, in richness and dazzling variety of colours, vied with all the perfection of oriental splendour.

armed with art, is able to distinguish land from sky; including the counties of SURREY and SUSSEX; part of HAMPSHIRE and BERKSHIRE; *Nettlebed* in OXFORDSHIRE; some parts of BUCKS, HERTFORDSHIRE, MIDDLESEX, KENT, and ESSEX; and WILTSHIRE.—The sea is discernible upwards of thirty miles distance, and, by the assistance of a glass, a vessel has actually been seen sailing! The numerous fields in the vale appear like so many beds in a garden, displaying all the various hues of green, yellow, russet, and dark brown. The great extent of wood-scenery, and the wilds, in the immediate vicinity of the hill, tend to darken the scene, whilst, in another part, the lively green of pasture lands serves to relieve their sombre effect.

Box-Hill, viewed from hence, loses all its importance, and appears like an insignificant spot; whilst the richly-clothed hills of Norbury, and the opposite chain, form a beautiful perspective of that romantic picturesque valley.

K

The view of a great city is always imposing and interesting. It gives rise to a multitude of associations, which never fail to present us with an immeasurable theatre of reflection. The contrast of our crowded and overgrown metropolis at twenty-five miles distance, with the calmness and placidity of the neighbouring country, made me exclaim with the poet :

> Here let me sweep
> The boundless landscape: now the raptured eye,
> Exulting swift, to huge AUGUSTA send;
> Now to the *sister-hills* that skirt her plain,
> To lofty *Harrow* now, and now to where
> Majestic *Windsor* lifts his princely brow,
> In lovely contrast to this glorious view,
> Calmly magnificent:
> * * * *
> Heavens! what a goodly prospect spreads around,
> Of hills, and dales, and woods, and lawns, and spires,
> ——————————— till all
> The stretching landscape into mist decays.
> *Thomson.*

Leith-Hill Tower, which stands upon one of the points of this delightful eminence, was built by Richard Hull, esq., in 1766, for a prospect-house: it formerly comprised two rooms, neatly furnished, and provided with glasses, for the accommodation of visitors. On the death of its founder, it was grievously neglected; insomuch, that, in a short time after, the floors, windows, &c. were left at the disposal of any one who stood in need of those materials. The consequence was, that it soon became a mere skeleton, or shell; but the gentlemen in the neighbourhood, wishing to preserve so conspicuous an object, caused the interior to be filled up with lime and rubbish, and nearly twenty feet, with the battlement and stone coping, to be added. These expences were defrayed by public subscription, in the year 1800. Over the door in the west front, is a stone, with the following (now inapplicable) inscription:

Ut terram undique beatam
Videas viator
Hæc turris de longe spectabilis
Sumptibus Richardi Hull
Ex agro Leith Hill Place Armig[ri].
Regnante Georgio Tertio
Anno Dom. MDCCLXVI.

Extructa fuit,
Oblectamento non sui solum
Sed Vicinorum
Et Omnium.

Within the tower, against the east wall, was a Portland stone (now dashed to pieces), containing an inscription, which is here preserved:

" Underneath this floor lieth the body of
Richard Hull, esq.
a native of Bristol,
who departed this life, January 18, 1772, in the 83d year of his age.

He was the eldest bencher of the Inner Temple, and served many years in the parliament of Ireland, where, by probity and vigilance, he zealously supported the interests of his constituents, and, after a long and faithful service in that station, he retired from the exercise of public to the enjoyment of private virtues; the testimony of a good conscience being his reward. He was a person eminent for the accomplishments of his mind and the purity of his heart. He lived, in the earlier part of his life, in habits of intimacy with Pope, Trenchard, Bishop Berkeley, and many other shining characters of those times; and, to wear off the remainder of his days, he purchased Leith Hill Place for a retirement, where he led the life of a rural philosopher; and, by his particular desire and direction, his remains are here deposited in a private manner, under this tower, which he erected a few years before his death."

I regretted, in common with every one who visits Leith-Hill, that so important a monument of public-spirited liberality should be utterly neglected by the descendants of its founder, and suffered to become little better than a public obloquy.* Meeting with a man who had assisted in building the tower, I ascertained from him that it was formerly much resorted to during the summer, and that he had frequently seen between thirty and forty private carriages here in one day. The number of visitors, of course, declined on the destruction of the prospect-rooms; and, the custom of frequenting watering-places being gradually introduced into the fashionable circles, Leith-Hill may now be said to be almost deserted.

Some well-intentioned individuals, however, endeavoured to re-establish this

---

* The walls of the tower have lately been much mutilated and defaced; it being the favourite practice of a few wanton urchins in the neighbourhood to resort thither on Sundays, and amuse themselves by pulling down great masses of the brick-work!

spot in popular favour, by proposing to hold an annual fair on the highest point of the hill. The attempt was, accordingly, first made in the summer of 1819, and on that interesting occasion, the hill presented a delightful picture of rural mirth. Hundreds of persons, of both sexes, dressed in their holiday clothes, flocked hither from all parts of the adjacent country; and many of them even came from a considerable distance, to participate in the festivities of the day. Every description of vehicle was put into requisition, from the elegant family carriage, to the humble market-cart. The day proved unusually fine. A band of music attended from Dorking. Booths and marquees were erected; but the simplicity of the scene was not destroyed by the multifarious exhibitions which usually attend on such occasions. Towards evening, the parties who detached themselves from the crowd, were, in a picturesque point of view, highly interesting. On the area of the tower, several sets were seen amusing themselves on the light fantastic toe; near to them were half-harnessed horses, feeding at their artificial mangers; and, in the descent of the hill, several parties were seen drinking tea, and taking refreshments, with a peculiar zest, not to be enjoyed even in the most splendid *salle-à-manger* of the wealthy and the great.

In short, this novel and amusing scene may be said to have resembled the village festival, in all its primeval simplicity; before the fraud and knavery of crowded cities had sent forth their despicable agents to cajole and corrupt the unsophisticated amusements of rural life.

The fair was not actually authorized by charter: certain abuses were said to have been committed, which called forth a public notice, prohibiting another fair being held; but it is truly painful to reflect, that the degeneracy of society should exist in so alarming an extent, as to require the interference of public authority, on occasions, which have their origin in the diffusion of rational enjoyment among all classes of the people.

Leith-Hill-Place, on the southern slope of the hill, is a small neat mansion; which was altered, into its present form, by Lieutenant-General Folliott. On his death, in 1748, this estate was purchased by Richard Hull, esq.* The house is placed in a retired situation, environed with woods and plantations, and is now in the occupation of the Rev. George Keylock Rusden.

Beyond Leith-Hill-Place, is *Tankurst*, commanding a beautiful and extensive prospect to the south. This residence was formerly the retreat of the lamented Sir Samuel Romilly, one of the able and inflexible representatives of Westminster. Thither Sir Samuel sometimes retired

---

* On enquiry among the peasantry in the neighbourhood, as to the character of this gentleman, an old woman described him as very liberal to the poor; but an *odd sort of a gentleman*. She also well recollected the day of his interment within the tower.

from the bustle and hum of public life, and enjoyed many hours in the delightful rides and walks of this neighbourhood. The lamentable intelligence of the death of Sir Samuel and Lady R. was received with the deepest regret by the poor of this district, who, at all times, bore testimony to the benevolence and urbanity of that enlightened statesman and his amiable lady. Tanhurst is now in the occupation of John A. Ogilvie, esq.

At the foot of Leith-Hill, is *Coldharbour*, supposed to be remains of an antient city, now reduced to a few straggling cottages. Among these, a modern brick building arrests the attention. This is a public school for the education of the poor children of the neighbourhood, and affords a pleasing proof of the progress of intellectual improvement in the humbler classes of society. The flourishing underwoods which border on Coldharbour, and here and there embosom a farm-house, or cottage, complete the romantic character of this dell. Paths winding on the margin of steep banks, and intersecting the woody track, resemble so many bye passes, which, together with the summit of Anstiebury Camp, bring into recollection all the historical data of days of yore.

Beyond Coldharbour, lies the small village of *Ockley*, on the antient Roman road Stane Street, which, for nearly three miles, in this parish, is still used as the common high road. The village is principally situated on a pleasant green; and received its name from the great quantity of oaks which grow here. The manor, which in the time of the Conqueror was held by Richard de Tonbridge, is now the property of Lee Steere Steere, esq., the representative of an opulent and honourable family, of great antiquity. Mr. Steere resides at *Jayes*, a short distance from Ockley-green, on which estate he has recently completed a noble mansion, where he supports the character of the country gentleman with the genuine spirit of English hospitality. There are, likewise, several handsome residences in the parish; among which are *Elderslie Lodge*, the residence of Capt. Sykes, R. N.; *Ockley Court*, the property of Charles Calvert, esq., M.P. for Southwark; and the Rectory House.

Ockley is remarkable as having been the field of the memorable defeat of the Danes, by Ethelwolf and his son, Athelstan. Thither the Danes fled, after having sacked London: the Saxon chronicle places this engagement in 851; Leland, in his Collections, in 873; and Milton between 851 and 853. The custom of planting and decorating the graves, once prevailed in the church-yard. Aubrey says, "hereabout the people draw peeled rushes through melted grease, which yields a sufficient light for ordinary use, is very cheap and useful, and burns long." This oeconomical method is still practised in the lower part of Surrey and Sussex.

I reluctantly left Leith-hill, by a winding chalky path, and turned off about a mile east of the tower, to a beautiful hill, supposed to be a Roman encampment, being in a direct line to the Stane Street, and known by the name of *Hanstie Bury*, that is the burg, hill, or fortress on the *Hean Stige*, or high road. The traces of this fortress, are very apparent; being nearly of a circular form, surrounded with a double trench, except on the south-east, south, and south-west, where the precipice rendered it unnecessary; and inclosing an area of eleven acres, one rood, and six perches, having the principal entrance on the north-east. Mr. Manning is inclined, from its circular form, to consider it as the work of the Danes; and it is said to have been their encampment previous to the sanguinary contest at Ockley, and where they planted their battering engines, with which they threw down Ockley castle. The heads of arrows, made of flint, in the form of a heart, and about an inch and a half in length, have frequently been found here.

North of this hill, the high land of the eastern acclivity, which is one mile in length, is covered with large coppices or woodlands, the part next Dorking being the summit. This track, called Red Land, and part of the Holmwood hills, is thickly planted with fir and chesnut trees, intersected by several circuitous walks; and, with Anstiebury,* is part of the entailed property of the late Duke of Norfolk, now granted on lease to Frederick Arnaud Clarke, esq. The area of Anstiebury is a delightful grove of larch, Scotch firs, and other forest trees. Mr. Clarke has lately placed several rustic seats on the borders of the paths, which wind in every direction, and frequently burst on variegated and striking prospects of the country beneath.

The descent from Anstiebury is by

---

* Anstiebury is the modern corruption of Hanstic Bury.

Boar-Hill, where, according to tradition, there were formerly wild boars. From hence, I crossed off to the waste, or common, called "The Holmwood," which was antiently, as the name implies, a *wood*. This immense tract was inhabited several centuries ago by a family called "de la Homewoode." In the survey of 1649, the Holmwood is described as being one of the wastes of the manor of Dorking, and then containing 796 acres; but, in records of greater antiquity, it is described as the wood of the Earls of Warren, the antient lords of the manor.

The common is pleasingly diversified with hill and dale, and interspersed with several neat cottages, with orchards, &c.: it is nearly covered with fern, holly-bushes, and furze, but many parts furnish good pasture. The western side is flanked by well-wooded heights, and to the east there is an interesting view of the country towards Reigate. The latter tract of country is said to have formed the retreat of the antient Britons, "whom the Romans could never drive out;" and, afterwards, it afforded a similar retreat to the Saxons, when the Danes ravaged the country in all directions. On this occasion, the following proverbial distich is attributed to them by Camden:

> " The Vale of Holmesdale,
> Never wonne, ne never shall."

Defoe says, " in the woody part of Holmward, or Holmesdale, are often found outlying red deer; and in the days of James II., or while he was Duke of York, they have hunted the largest stags here that have been seen in England." He also says, " The Holmward was once famous for producing such qualities of strawberries, that they were carried to market by horse-loads." There are several farms of considerable antiquity in this neighbourhood, most of which receive their names from their former proprietors. A gate adjoining the Worthing road leads by a private road to *Henfold*, the late residence of Charles Duke of Norfolk, which is now let on lease to F. A. Clarke, esq., who resides at a neat cottage and sporting-box on the same estate, in the enjoyment of extensive manorial rights and privileges. The spacious mansion was built of Charlwood granite, by the late duke, but has not been completed; and it is now occupied only by *owls* and *foxes*, which abound in this neighbourhood. The late duke commenced building this noble pile in 1807, on the brow of an eminence near Ewood, formerly surrounded by a park of 600 acres, in which was a fine sheet of water; intending to make Henfold his occasional residence, being at an equal distance from the metropolis and Arundel Castle. The house is placed in the midst of a thick wood, and presents a pleasing object in the prospect from the neighbouring hills. The estate abounds with commanding eminences, and all the rich and varied charms of sylvan scenery; intersected by innumerable bye-paths, which wind through several retired glades, and occasionally burst forth on the most enchanting prospects of the surrounding country; including, in one grand *coup-d'œil*, the woody heights of the Deepdene, Denbies, Handbridge, and Box-Hill.

On the western side of the road is *Broomhalls*, formerly the residence of a family, called from thence *de la Brome*. It is now the property of C. W. Collins, esq., who has considerably enlarged and improved the residence. In the same neighbourhood, also, is *Lyne*, the property of James Broadwood, esq., joint proprietor in the celebrated piano-forte manufactory in the metropolis. Aubrey says, "these parts were formerly so full of wood for firing, that it might be bought for threepence or fourpence per load, the buyer being at the expence of cutting and carriage."

Skirting the Holmwood, I at length arrived at Brockham-green, a tything, belonging to Betchworth, properly called Brookham, from being situated near the brook or river. On the borders of the green, are several cottage-residences.

Contiguous to the green, is *Brockham Court Lodge*, the delightful retreat of Captain Charles Morris, author of some of the finest lyrical ballads in our language. This gentleman, at an early period of life, distinguished himself by his devotion to the muses. Among the most popular of his political productions may be mentioned the celebrated ballad of " Billy's too young to drive us," and the song of " Billy Pitt and the Farmer;" which continued long in fashion, and were considered to be most faithful and humourous satires on the reigning politics of the day. His inestimable Anacreontic song, *Ad Poculum*, procured for him the gold cup from the Harmonic Society, some years since: and the following *morceau* will, doubtless, be considered too precious to be passed over by the votary of the lyric muse.

The old Whig Poet to his old Buff Waistcoat.

Farewell, thou poor rag of the muse!
  In the bag of the cloathsman go lie:
A sixpence thou'lt fetch from the Jews,
  Which the hard hearted Christians deny.
Twenty years, in adversity's spite,
  I bore thee most proudly along;
Stood jovially *buff* to the fight,
  And won the world's ear with my song.
But, prosperity's humbled thy case:
  Thy friends in full banquet I see,
And the door kindly shut in my face,
  Thou'st become a *fool's garment* to me!
Poor rag! thou art welcome no more,
  The days of thy *service* are past,
Thy toils and thy glories are o'er,
  And thou and thy master are *cast*.
But, though thou'rt forgot and betrayed,
  'Twill ne'er be forgotten by me,
How my old lungs within thee have play'd,
  And my spirits have swelled thee with glee.
Perhaps they could swell thee no more,
  For Time's icy hand's on my head;
My spirits are weary and sore,
  And the impulse of Friendship is dead.
Then adieu! tho' I cannot but fret
  That my constancy with thee most part,
For thou hast not a hole in thee yet,
  Though through *thee* they have wounded my heart.
I change thee for sable, more sage,
  To mourn the hard lot I abide;
And mark upon *gratitude's* page,
  A *blot* that hath buried my *pride*.
Ah! who would believe in these lands
  From the *Whigs* I should suffer a wrong?
Had they seen how with hearts and with hands
  They followed in frenzy my song.
Who'd have thought, though so eager their claws,
  They'd condemn me *thus hardly* to plead?
Through my *prime*, I have toiled for your cause
  And you've left me, when aged, in need,
Could ye not midst the favours of fate,
  Drop a mite where all own it is due?
Could ye not from the *feast* of the *state*
  Throw a *crumb* to a servant so true?
In your *scramble* I stirred not a jot,
  Too proud for rapacity's strife;
And sure that all hearts would allot
  A scrap to the *claims* of *my life*.
But go, faded rag, and while gone
  I'll turn thy hard fate to my ease;
For the hand of kind heaven hath shewn
  All crosses have colours that please.
Thus a *bliss* from thy shame I receive,
  Though my body's met treatment so foul,
I can suffer, forget, and forgive,
  And get comfort, more worth for my soul.
And when seen on the rag-seller's rope,
  They who know thee'll say ready enough
"There service hangs jilted by hope,
  "This once was poor Al---rr---le's buff."

> If they let them give virtue her name
> And yield an example to teach,
> Poor rag, thou hast served in thy *shame*
> Better ends than thy *honours* could reach.
> But, through the soul gain by the loss,
> The stomach and pocket still say,
> "Pray what shall we do in this cross?"
> I answer, "be *poor* and be gay."
> Let the mope gather mirth from her wrong,
> Smooth her wing in *adversity's shower;*
> To new ears and new hearts tune her song,
> And still look for a *sun-shining hour!*
> While I, a disbanded old Whig,
> Put up my discharge with a smile;
> Face about—prime and load—take a swig,
> And march off—to the opposite file.
>
> G. R. Aug. 1st. 1815.

Captain Morris has, for many years past, moved in the first society, and frequented the best company. His songs, "Political and Convivial," have passed through twenty-four editions, and will at all times add to the relish of the banquet by mirth, and heighten the charms of festivity by jollity. He is, also, well known in the convivial circles as having been the intimate friend and companion of a deceased illustrious nobleman, at whose table he was always a welcome guest.[*]

In this elegant and commodious villa, Capt. Morris usually passes the summer

---

[*] The father of Capt. Morris also possessed a poetical turn, and actually composed the popular song of *Kitty Crowder.*

months with his family.* His manners are those of a scholar and a gentleman; and the urbanity of his deportment ensures him respect and esteem, both as a gentleman of fortune, and of highly-cultivated talents. The gardens and bowery walks of this pleasing little estate seem well adapted for the retirement of a man of genius, and, amidst whose fairy scenes, Capt. M. enjoys many happy hours.

Beyond Brockham is the village of *Betchworth*, in which is the mansion of the Rt. Hon. Henry Goulburn. It was formerly the property of the Hon. W. H. Bouverie, and contained several fine por-

---

* No less than three generations of this family have all served in the army, and were by turns in the same regiment, of which one of them had the command. Capt. M. afterwards exchanged into the Horse Guards, where he was the contemporary of Capt. Topham. He has two sons in the army. The lady of the former (Major M.) it will be recollected, descended in a diving-bell at Plymouth, a short time since; on which occasion, she penned some very appropriate stanzas, while seated in the bell.

traits, and some antient statues. The residence was built in the time of James I. by Sir Ralph Freeman, who purchased this estate of the trustees of the Earl of Abergavenny. In the chimney-piece of the drawing-room is a piece of sculpture from Herculaneum, representing boys riding on bulls and horses.

Wonham, one of the manors in this parish, was purchased in 1787 by the Hon. Charles Marsham, the late Earl of Romney. He rebuilt the house on a larger scale than before; and on his accession to the title sold it to John Stables, esq. who, in 1804, disposed of it to Viscount Templetown. The grounds comprehend 120 acres, including a park of sixty-six, which is in part bounded by the Mole.

In Upper Betchworth is *Broom*, the tasteful residence of William Kenrick, esq. On the east is a lawn, surrounded with fine plantations. The grounds are well watered by ponds, supplied from a spring which rises in the neighbourhood.

In the plantations near the road, formerly stood a mill for sawing boards, containing twenty-two saws, which were worked by a stream. It was erected by C. Kilby, esq., formerly proprietor of this villa, who, also, built a curious edifice, called *the Priory*, and several other ornamental seats, &c.* Beyond Broom, is the village of *Buckland*, whence the road winds off to Reigate.

From Brockham-green, I proceeded to *Betchworth Castle*. At the General Survey, the manor belonging to this estate formed part of the possessions of Richard de Tonbridge, and afterwards of the Earls of Arundel. In 1377 John Fitz Alan, second son of Richard, Earl of Arundel, having succeeded to this estate, had license to embattle his manor-house here. A similar license was granted to Thomas Brown, esq.; he had permission,

---

* This enchanting spot was formerly called *Tranquil Dale*, and its situation truly corresponds with that appellation; being consecrated, as it were, to the lovers of rural quiet and contemplation.

also, to impark his manor, and have free warren in the same. The estate continued in the family of Browne, until the death of Sir Adam, in 1690, when it devolved to his sole daughter, married to W. Fenwick, esq., who pulled down the greater part of the castle, and altered the remainder into a dwelling-house. Mrs. Fenwick was the last of the Brownes, who had been owners of this estate nearly 300 years. On her death, it was sold in 1727, to Abraham Tucker, esq., the author of an excellent work on metaphysics, entitled the *Light of Nature pursued*, published under the signature of A. Search, esq. At his death, in 1774, the estate descended to his youngest daughter, who bequeathed it to Sir Henry Paulet St. John Mildmay, who, in 1798, sold the whole property to Henry Peters, esq. banker, of London, the present owner.[*]

---

[*] This gentleman filled the office of high-sheriff of Surrey, in 1817; and is a partner in the flourishing banking concern of Messrs. Masterman and Co. of White-hart court, Lombard-street.

The castle is seated on an eminence, on the western bank of the river Mole. It has a handsome and venerable appearance, for which it is greatly indebted to the taste of its present owner, who has made considerable improvements in the buildings and grounds; and has enlarged the estate by extensive purchases. The situation of this residence is one of the most delightful that can possibly be imagined. Environed on all sides with lawns, tastefully-arranged gardens, shrubbery-walks, and banks thickly clothed with luxuriant evergreens, it forms one of the most enchanting retreats of this country. The detached offices of the establishment exhibit great taste in their construction; the style of rural architecture rendering them both useful and ornamental appendages. Every department is planned on the completest scale, and well accords with the importance and respectability of its present and former proprietor.

The park is remarkable for the stately

timber with which it is adorned. Approaching the castle from Dorking, the road leads through an outer park, skirted with rows of old chesnut-trees, of large dimensions; and the inner, at the extremity of which the castle is situated, has two fine avenues, the one of elms, and the other, 850 yards in length, composed of a triple row of limes of gigantic size and height. The last avenue resembles the nave of a cathedral: the trees form on the outside a vast screen or wall of verdure; within, the branches, meeting at a great height in the air from the opposite rows, form Gothic arches, and exclude every ray of the meridian sun. The river Mole, washing the verdant edge of the park, has in some parts an important breadth, and is thickly shaded with aquatic trees and bushes.

From Betchworth Castle, I crossed the park, over a rich succession of beautiful lawny slopes and eminences, and in my route passed an elegant summer-house, fitted up with great taste, and commanding a fascinating prospect of the Holmesdale. Journeying southward, I soon reached *Chart Park,* in which formerly stood a neat mansion. The last owner and resident was the late Sir Charles Talbot, bart., by whose devisees it was sold to Thomas Hope, esq. the proprietor of the Deepdene, who pulled down the house and offices, and annexed the grounds to his own estate.

The park was formed by Henry Talbot, esq., fourth son of Dr. W. Talbot, Bishop of Durham, and youngest surviving brother of Lord Talbot, Lord High Chancellor of England. The house in his time was but small: it stood directly at the foot of the steep hill, on the north of the park, on the side of which hill was a *Vineyard,* supposed to have been planted by the Hon. Charles Howard; who, it is said, erected the residence (as it were) in the vineyard, there being no house here previously to his residing at the Deepdene. The vineyard flourished for some time, and tolerably good wine was made from the produce; but, after the death of the noble planter, in 1713, it was much neglected, and nothing remained but the name, which was retained until Mr. Talbot came into possession, when he gave to the estate the appellation of *Chart Park*.* On taking down the house, a

---

* At the extremity of the Chart grounds, Mr. HOPE has erected a spacious family *mausoleum*, capable of containing upwards of twenty bodies. Two of his sons, who died in their youth, are buried here.

Many of the wisest and best of men have signalized their love of gardens and shrubberies, by causing themselves to be buried in them. PLATO was buried in the groves of Academus: SIR WILLIAM TEMPLE gave orders for his heart to be enclosed in a silver casket, and placed under a sun-dial, opposite his library window: DERCENNUS, one of the kings of Latium, was buried in a thick wood, on the top of a high mountain: ROUSSEAU was buried in the Island of Poplars, in the gardens of Ermenonville: HORNE TOOKE was buried in his own garden: and NAPOLEON BONAPARTE often walked to a fountain in the island of St. Helena, and said to his confidential companions, "*If it is destined that I die on this rock, let me be buried in this place,*" pointing to some willows near the fountain he so frequently visited.

stone resembling a mill-stone was found, by which the grapes were pressed. The series of irregular heights which compose the southern side of this vale, leads next to an eminence marked by a clump of firs, and commonly called DORKING'S GLORY. This is a most happy station for a prospect, commanding not only the vales of Letherhead and Dorking, but a long tract of the southern part of Surrey, extending to the borders of Sussex.

Close behind the site of the house, the ground rises abruptly to a terrace, planted with a line of beeches. Here is also a neat stone pediment, supported by two pillars, on the former of which is inscribed

FRATRI OPTVMO.

Beneath the pediment is a stone seat, from which the picturesque valley of REIGATE, backed by well-wooded hills, presents a scene of no ordinary character.

This simply-elegant architectural ornament is placed against a boundary wall, on the other side of which is the *Deep-*

dene, the classical estate of Thomas Hope, esq. From this spot the panorama of the surrounding country includes all the captivating charms of Box-Hill, Norbury-Park, Denbies, and the Guildford-hills; and the pleasant little common, Cotmandene, adjoining the vale immediately beneath.

Aubrey gives the following original and interesting account of his visit to this estate:

"Near this place, (Dorking,) the Hon. Charles Howard, of Norfolk, hath very ingeniously contrived a *long hope,* * (i. e. according to Virgil, *Deductus vallis*) in the most pleasant and delightful solitude, for house, gardens, orchards, boscages, &c. that I have seen in England: it deserves a poem, and was a subject worthy of Mr. Cowley's muse. The true name of this Hope is Dibden (quasi Deepdene.)"

"Mr. Howard hath cast this hope into the form of a theatre, on the sides whereof he hath made several narrow walks, like the seats of a theatre, one above another, above six in number, done with a plough, which are bordered with thyme, and some cherry-trees, myrtles, &c. Here were a great many orange-trees and syringas, which

---

* A *hope* is described to be the side of a hill, or low ground amidst hills.

were then in flower. In this time are twenty-one sorts of thyme. The pit, (as I may call it) is stored full of rare flowers and choice plants. He hath there two pretty lads, his gardeners, who wonderfully delight in their occupation; and this lovely solitude, and do enjoy themselves so innocently in that pleasant corner, as if they were out of this troublesome world, and seem to live as in the state of innocency."

"In the hill on the left hand, (being sandy ground,) is a cave digged thirty-six paces long, four broad, and five yards high; and at about two-thirds of the hill, (where the crook or bowing is) he hath dug another subterranean walk or passage,* to be pierced through the hill; through which (as through a tube) you have the visto over all the south part of Surrey and Sussex to the sea. The south side of this hill is converted into a vineyard of

---

* This work was never completed, as appears by Manning's Account, although any one might infer from Aubrey that it was so.

Salmon, speaking of the project, says, "They tell us at Dorking of a scheme about fifty years since, and not out of the memory of the oldest, for cutting a hypogæum through Deepdene-hill. It was to have been from the north side, which lies next the mansion-house and Betchworth castle, and to have opened on the concave side of the hill, in what they call the theatre or vineyard. To this purpose labourers were employed, who had carried on their mine from both ends a considerable way, in order to meet in the middle: but, for want of arch or support, the earth fell in near one end, which put an end to the design. The miners were come out to breakfast, so that nothing but their tools were covered."

many acres of ground, which faceth the south and south-west."

"On the west side of this garden is a little building, which is (as I remember) divided into a laboratory and a neat oratory, by Mr. Howard. Above the hill, on this west side, is a thicket of black cherry-trees; and the walks and the grounds abound with strawberries. The house was not made for grandeur, but retirement (a noble hermitage); neat, elegant, and suitable to the modesty and solitude of the proprietor, a christian philosopher, who, in this iron age, lives up to that of the primitive times. Here Mr. Newman (his steward,) gave me a very civil entertainment, according to his master's order; where the pleasures of the garden, &c. were so ravishing that I can never expect any enjoyment beyond it but the kingdom of heaven. It is an agreeable surprize here to the stranger, that neither house nor garden can be discovered till you come just at it, as if it squatted down to hide itself."

"In short, this estate is an epitome of paradise, and the garden of Eden seems well imitated here. To give my reader a just notion of this is almost impossible."

Salmon, in describing the Deepdene, gives the following curious conjectures as to the antiquity of this spot:

"If we were to search through the island for a place to perform the religious rites of the Celts, nothing comes up to the amphitheatre of Deepden, adjoining to Cotmandene. I will not say there are any vestigia of their sacrifices, but the place by nature is so surprisingly contrived for worship, or theatrical entertainment, as if it had been cut out of the hill by human hands. The figure of it tempted the honourable Mr. Howard to turn it into a vineyard, and to grace it with all the variety planting and gardening could add. 'Tis at present woody on the north side to the top, and, probably, was such antiently on the concave side. No Druid could see this beauty neglected, nor doubt that nature had formed it for the adoration of the Deity, where sacrifice might be performed with the greatest solemnity, the scene commanding the veneration of the people, and the capacious theatre containing a greater number than ever attended a shew of gladiators. On both sides this romantick place, stand hills of vast height, and beautiful aspect. Box-hill, and that of Mr. Tryon's warren,* on the north; on the south, White-Down and Lithe-hill. Leith is a corruption of Lithe, signifying *long*, which this hill corresponds with."

"What is said upon this being merely conjecture, and without that degree of evidence we have generally for Roman antiquities, I pursue it no further, than that Cotmonden by the general voice of the neighbourhood, is called the best air in England. 'Tis much such an observation should be made for a spot of twenty acres, unless something antiently had contributed to it. If Deepdene was a place of British or Saxon worship, some healthful virtue might be imagined to overspread the verge."

I descended from the terrace of Chart-Park into the *long hope*, or vale, as before

---

* Norbury Park.

described. Here I was much gratified with a pleasing picture of landscape-gardening; the quiet of echoing dells; and the refreshing coolness of caves and subterranean passages, all which combined to render this spot a kind of FAIRY REGION. Flower-gardens, laid out in parterres, with much taste, here mingle the aspect of trim neatness with rude uncultivated nature, in walks winding through woods and plantations, and containing several ruined grottoes and hermitages, well adapted, by their solitary situations, to study and reverie. The gardens are tastefully embellished with some elegant casts, and in the midst of them are small basins of water.

Nearly adjoining the caverns is a neat tablet, with the following verses, written by Lady Burrell, the authoress of several other poems.

"This votive tablet is inscribed to the memory of the Honourable Charles Howard, who built an oratory and laboratory on this spot: he died at the Deepdene, 1714.

If worth, if learning, should with fame be crown'd,
  If to superior talents, fame be due,
Let *Howard's* virtues consecrate the ground
  Where once the fairest flowers of science grew.

Within this calm retreat, th' illustrious sage
  Was wont his grateful orisons to pay,
Here he perused the legendary page,
  Here gave to chemistry the feeling day.

Cold to ambition, far from courts remov'd,
  Though qualified to fill the statesman's part,
He studied nature in the paths he lov'd,
  Peace in his thoughts, and virtue in his heart.

Soft may the breeze sigh through the ivy boughs
  That shade this humble record of his worth;
Here may the robin undisturb'd repose,
  And fragrant flowers adorn the hallow'd earth.
                                    January, 1792.

This romantic estate descended to the last Duke of Norfolk but one, who pulled down the old house, and built the present noble mansion in its stead. His duchess was very fond of the gardens, and formed a hermitage here, with all the humble requisites for a holy anchorite. The last duke sold the place in 1791, to the late Sir William Burrell, bart., who died in

1796. His lady resided here until her death, when the estate descended to Sir Charles Burrell, bart., who sold the whole property to Thomas Hope, esq., the present possessor.

Mr. Hope, it will be recollected, has applied the fine arts, with judgment, to the internal decoration of houses; and, has already published an important work on that subject, besides two works on antient and modern costume.* Mr. Hope has, however, lately re-appeared before the literary world, in a work which at once places him in the highest list of eloquent writers and superior men—viz. Anastasius; or the Memoirs of a Modern Greek. There are, indeed, few books in the English language which contain passages of greater power, feeling, and eloquence, than this novel,—which delineate frailty and vice with more energy and acuteness,

---

* It should not be forgotten, that to the liberality of Mr. Hope, THORVALSDEN, the celebrated sculptor, is chiefly indebted for support and patronage.

or describe historical scenes with such bold imagery and such glowing language.* Contemporary criticism has universally allowed it to be a work in which great and extraordinary talent is evinced. It abounds in eloquent and sublime passages,—in sense,—in knowledge of history, and in knowledge of human character; —and a rapid sale of three large editions has proved these superior characteristics to have been amply recognized by the literary public.

The Deepdene has been considerably improved and embellished by Mr. Hope; and these improvements have not been confined to in-door comforts or additions. The grounds exhibit much taste, and un-

---

* The Edinburgh Reviewers, with a degree of pleasantry and causticity peculiar to those veterans in criticism, ask "Where has Mr. Hope hidden all his eloquence and poetry up to this hour?—How is it that he has, all of a sudden, burst out into descriptions, which would not disgrace the pen of Tacitus—and displayed a depth of feeling and vigour of imagination which Lord Byron could not excel? We do not shrink from one syllable of this eulogy."

ceasing variety in their disposal; and, in truth, every portion of the estate abounds with proofs of the highly-cultivated genius and talent of their worthy proprietor. Ornamental bridges, porticoes, lodges, green-houses, orangeries, pineries, gates, and even rustic seats, here have some peculiarity, which denotes they were designed by no ordinary taste. These features, combined with the beauties of a natural amphitheatre, (whose sides are embrowned with woods and rocks,) successively present the most inviting scenes for the luxury of meditation, and the bewitching revelry of rapture and thought.

As a patron of the many important institutions, and public improvements in this parish, Mr. Hope is a liberal contributor; and the poor of the neighbourhood will cheerfully acknowledge him as one of their warmest benefactors. The interior of the mansion is very superbly fitted up, and contains several rare productions of the fine arts. The family occasionally retire thither from the metropolis, where they have a splendid residence in Mansfield-street, and a valuable gallery of pictures, by masters of the first celebrity; which may be inspected through the courtesy of their proprietor. Mr. Hope possesses immense wealth, and, it is but justice to say, he dispenses it with princely munificence.

I left the Deepdene by a gate opening to the Reigate-road, where I caught a view of *Pipbrook House*, the seat of W. Crawford, esq., and so called from its being on the bank of the stream of that name. The residence is a plain stuccoed building, and the adjacent grounds are arranged with much neatness.

From hence I crossed several beautiful meadows, and passed a neat residence, and a flour-mill on the banks of the river Mole. This path leads, through some fields, to the angle of the Reigate road. A bye-road, branching off to the left, winds over Box-Hill, to the villages of Headley and Walton; and a foot-path crosses the side of the hill, and ascends to the summit.

This celebrated eminence is situated in the north range of chalk hills, beginning near *Farnham*, in this county, and extending from thence to *Folkstone*, in Kent. Its greatest elevation is over against the Grove, which is 445 feet perpendicular from the level of the Mole. Adjoining Box-Hill, on the east, is *Brockham-Hill*, on which is a clump of trees, 162 feet higher than the woody part of Box-Hill. On the top is a farm-yard: and it is a remarkable circumstance that, from a spring here, water is obtained at only fifteen feet from the surface of the ground, though at Denbies, on the opposite hill, it is drawn from the depth of 400 feet.

Box-hill receives its name from the quantity of box-wood growing on it. Camden, speaking of it, calls it *White-Hill*, from its chalky soil, particularly at the part towards Burford Bridge; but Box-Hill is its true and antient name. It has been

ROUND DORKING. 233

asserted by writers, that the box was planted by Thomas Earl of Arundel, between two and three centuries ago; but there is authentic evidence of its being there long before his time: in all probability, the tree is the natural produce of the soil. Indeed, this hill was never the Earl's property. *Henry de Buxeto* [i.e. Henry of Box-Hill,] and *Adam de Buxeto* were witnesses to deeds as early as the reign of King John or Henry III.

Aubrey, speaking of Box-Hill, says:

"One part, north of this hill, is covered with yew-trees in great plenty, and the best that I have any where seen.* The south part is covered with thick boscages of box-trees, which gives the name to this hill.

"I am told that, on this hill, juniper-trees have been in great plenty:† now they are much worn out.

"From this hill, southward, is a large view‡ over the

---

* This part of the hill belongs to the Ashurst estate, the property of A. Strahan, esq. the King's printer. The yews were mostly cut down by Mr. Robert Boxall, who purchased the estate in the year 1780.

† Mickleham Downs, adjoining this hill, abound with many of these trees.

‡ In "*England's Gazetteer*," by Philip Luckombe, the

Wyld of Surrey, (which is about seven miles,) to the Downs in Sussex, and to the *town of Dorking*, which is situated in the angle of two pretty valleys; westwards, to *Hampshire, Berks,* and *Oxfordshire;* in which last may be discerned a tuft of trees on a hill, which I guess to be *Nettlebed;* and to another hill, northwards, towards Windsor, viz. *Cowper's-Hill* in Middlesex.

"The soil is chalk, and was the inheritance of Sir Adam Browne, now Mr. Fenwick's. The great quantity and thickness of the box-wood yielded a convenient privacy for lovers, who frequently meet here; so that it is an *English Daphne*. The gentry often resorted here from *Bibisham*; but the wood is much decayed now, and huge depredations have been made on it by the present possessor, (Mr. Fenwick,) who is only a tenant for his life. The hill runs continuedly from hence to Kent, and so to Dover; it is interrupted by the little valley, and so runs by Guildford town. On the South Downs of this county, and in those of Sussex, are the biggest snails that ever I saw, twice or

---

following notice is taken of this hill:—"There is a large warren upon it, but no houses; only arbours, cut out in the box-wood on the top of the hill, where are sold refreshments of all sorts, for the gentlemen and ladies who come hither to divert themselves in its labyrinths; for which reason a certain author has thought fit to call it the PALACE OF VENUS, and also the TEMPLE OF NATURE; there being an enchanting prospect from it of a fine country, which is scarce to be equalled, for affording so surprising and magnificent an idea both of earth and sky." This is probably extracted from some other writer.

three times as big as our common snails, which are the *Bavoli*, or *Drivalle*; which Mr. Elias Ashmole tells me, that the Lord Marshal* brought from Italy, and scattered them on the Downs hereabouts, and between Albury and Horsley, where are the biggest of all."

The box-trees on the hills are much thinned, from frequent and general cutting; although at this time they are recovering, as they have been untouched for the last few years. The box-wood has at various times produced the proprietors of this estate a great profit. In an account rendered to Ambrose, the son of Sir Matthew Browne, by his guardian, the receipt for one year, to Michaelmas 1608, for box-trees, cut down upon the sheep-walk on this hill, is £50. In an account of West Betchworth Manor, taken in 1712, it is supposed that as much had

---

* This was one of the Earls of Arundel and Earls Marshal. It is, probably, from this small account, that the error, ascribing the planting of the box to one of the Earls of Arundel, has arisen. The snails were brought thither for the Countess of Arundel, who was accustomed to dress and eat them for a consumptive complaint.

been cut down, within a few years before, as amounted to £3000.*

I wandered amidst the groves and trackless paths of this *elysium*, until the

---

* Insignificant as this shrub appears, it has been to its owners a source of considerable profit. But the ships from the Levant brought such quantities of it in ballast, that the wood on the hill could not find a purchaser, and, not having been cut for sixty-five years, was growing cankered. The war diminished the influx from the Mediterranean; several purchasers offered; and, in 1795, Sir H. Mildmay put it up by auction at £12,000. The depredations made on Box-Hill, in consequence of this sale, did not injure its picturesque beauty, as it is twelve years in cutting, which gives each portion a reasonable time to renew.—*Gilpin.*

" These trees rise naturally," says Evelyn, " in Kent, at Bexley; and in Surrey, giving name to Box-Hill. He that, in winter, should behold some of our highest hills in Surrey clad with whole woods of them, for divers miles in circuit, as in those delicious groves of them belonging to the late Sir Adam Browne, of Betchworth Castle, might easily fancy himself transported into some new or enchanted country." The enchantment, alas! has been long broken. Mr. Miller, in 1759, lamented that the trees on Box-Hill had been then pretty much destroyed; though many remained of considerable bigness. The destruction since that time has been much greater. Not only this hill near Dorking, in Surrey and Bexley in Kent, but all-glorious sun shed his magnificent rays over the delightful scene. Beneath me lay extended a tract of country, which has been aptly termed " THE GARDEN OF SURREY;" and includes, in one splendid panorama, all the congregated charms of the valley through which I had been journeying.

A stump of wood, rising from one of the prominent points of the hill, denotes the burial-place of Major Labelliere, an officer in the Marines. This gentleman,

---

Boxwell in Coteswold, Gloucestershire, was named from this tree. Mr. Woodward remarks it as plentiful on the chalk-hills near Dunstable.

The English wood is esteemed inferior to that which comes from the Levant; and the American box is said to be preferable to ours.

The Romans clipped box into form, for which nothing is more fit, says Pliny: " *Ut quæ (arbor) ob densè subnascentes surculos et frondes, in animalium aliorumve effigies componi et detonderi præ alia quæcunque apta est.*" And Martial observes of the garden at Bassus's country-house:
———*otiosis ordinata myrtetis,*
Viduaque Platano, tonsilique buxeto.
Encyclop. Londinensis.

in early life, fell in love with a lady, who, although he was remarkably handsome in person, eventually rejected his addresses; a circumstance which could not fail to inflict a deep wound on his delicate mind. It was not, however, till many years after, that his reason became actually obscured. At this time, the late Duke of Devonshire, who had formerly been very fond of his company, allowed him a pension of £100. a-year for life.

He resided at Chiswick, whence he frequently walked to London, followed by a tribe of ragged boys, whom he would occasionally harangue; both his pockets being, generally, filled, to an overflow, with newspapers and political pamphlets. From Chiswick he came to settle at Dorking; where, from his utter inattention to common cleanliness, he acquired the appellation of " the walking dunghill." Numerous are the anecdotes which might be quoted of his eccentricities. Among these is the following :—To a gentleman, with whom he was in habits of intimacy, he presented a parcel, curiously folded and sealed, with a particular injunction not to open it till after his death. This request was strictly complied with; but, on opening the packet, it was found to contain merely a plain memorandum-book.—By his own request, he was buried, without church-rites, on this beautiful eminence, with his head downwards; it being a constant assertion with him, "*that the world was turned topsy-turvy, and, therefore, at the end of it he should be right.*"

At the foot of this hill, the charming grounds of the Burford estate, and the Grove, present an interesting little *coup d'œil*, displaying their rich verdant lawns, studded with stately trees, and intersected with narrow winding paths. Beyond these delicious retreats is the pleasant neighbourhood of Westhumble. To the right, the prospect stretches away through the romantic vale of Norbury, to Letherhead, and the once-famed vicinity of Epsom;* and, in another direction, to the variegated country of Kingston, and the enchanting scenery of "Esher's groves." To the left, the delightful town and neighbourhood of Dorking appears, surrounded

---

* Mr. Toland gives the following vigorous description of this place:—

"You have resolved (as you do every thing) to purchase a summer retreat, cost what it will, somewhere in this neighbourhood. But, whether you gently step over my favourite meadows, planted on all sides quite to Woodcot seat, in whose long grove I oftenest converse with myself; or that you walk further on to Ashted house and park, the sweetest spot of ground in our British world; or ride still farther, the enchanted prospect of Box-Hill, that temple of nature, no-where else to be equalled for affording so surprising and magnificent an idea both of heaven and earth; whether you lose yourself in the aged yew-groves of Mickleham, as the river Mole does hide itself in the shallows beneath, or that you had rather try your patience in angling for trouts about Letherhead; whether you go to some cricket-match, or other prizes of contending villagers, or choose to breathe your horse at a race, and to follow a pack of hounds in the proper weather; whether, I say, you delight in any or every one of these, Epsom is the place you must like before all others."

by the woody heights of the Deepdene, Wotton, and Denbies, and the wild expanse of the Holmesdale and Leith-Hill; and, beyond these, the whole of Sussex, to the South Downs, at the distance of thirty-six miles!

In the magnificent scene viewed from this hilly pivot, the emulative handicraft of man had contrived to raise a few puny edifices, whose proud roofs were seen just overtopping the foliage of the surrounding woods. The day would, however, have been spent much more unprofitably in examining their interiors. There, perhaps, I might have beheld specimens of exquisitely-finished workmanship, and unique models of taste. Their walls and galleries might be hung with the matchless productions of eminent masters in the different schools, and profusely decorated by the magic pencil of art; and their libraries furnished more as ostentatious ornaments, than for their in-

M

trinsic value, and "whose very indices are not to be read over in an age."

The great error of mankind appears to be in overstraining *art*, and thus interdicting the endless variety of enjoyment which *nature* continually presents for the extension of our present comforts. A city, crammed with A MILLION of human beings, is thus preferred to the retirement of the country, merely because it is the grand mart for every commodity which industry and ingenuity can furnish. There, huddled together, creature is grappling with creature, in trafficking controversy. Thousands are pouring forth from crowded habitations, inhaling noxious vapours; others are sinking under their daily toil, from lassitude and bodily exhaustion: and there, perhaps, may be seen the wealthy and the great, whose villas are tenantless until the chilling damps of autumn shall have impaired the country of its meridian splendour. The country, at all seasons of the year, has its special pleasures to divert the mind, and, at the same time, to replenish it with useful knowledge.—" I never in my life," says Dennis, " left the country without regret, and always returned to it with joy. The sight of a mountain is more agreeable than that of the most pompous edifices; and meadows and naturally-winding streams please me before the most beautiful gardens and the most costly canals." THOUSANDS, who have emerged from the metropolis to visit the ELYSIUM OF BOX-HILL, have there reiterated these sentiments, with rapturous and soul-stirring ecstasy!

I now descended the steep, aided by the roots and clumps, to a winding walk overhung with foliage.* Here the silence of the scene was broken by the gentle tricklings of the river MOLE, which glides at the foot of the hill; about which so much cavil and controversy has been

---

* At each end of this walk is a locked gate, and a board stating it to be private property.

excited. Mr. Middleton, the agriculturist, says, "the Mole, like all other rivers, is carrying the finest and decomposed parts of the soil, which happen to lie in its course, towards the sea. Hence, the river washes the marl and sand from under a part of Box-Hill and the adjoining meadows. In this manner, cavities and under-ground passages are made; and the similitude of the place to the labours of the mole, has been the occasion of naming the river. Into these cavities, many patches of the super-strata (or meadow-land of Mrs. Barclay) have sunk; and these places are called SWALLOWS."

Mr. Aubrey informs us, that, "in 1760, one night, by the road-side, fell down a great deal of earth on one side of the hill, and was a great pit of about thirty feet deep: at the bottom, they could discover water running over the earth sunk in." On the south side, about ninety yards east of the Hare and Hounds, three other pits, lying on the side of the hill near the road, proceeded from the same cause, though of an earlier date.

Salmon, in describing the Mole, says, "This river rises in St. Leonard's Forest, in Sussex, and is called the Mole, from a great part of the water sinking into the earth below the two bridges, and bursting out again near Letherhead." Pope, likewise, commemorates this river in his *Windsor Forest:*

"The sullen Mole, that dives his hiding flood."

I wandered through this rural paradise, which communicates with the pleasure-grounds of the *Hare and Hounds* inn, at the foot of the hill. At the end of a shady walk, which may be said to be a miniature representation of the Druid's, or Lover's Walk, at Vauxhall-Gardens, a small wooden bridge communicates with the Burford estate.* This

---

* In this part, the trunk of an aged tree extends across the river, and is often mentioned as the obstacle which occasioned the drowning of some adventurous gentlemen, who, some years ago, attempted to *navigate the Mole.* The water being high, the tree was hidden; when

walk opens into the lawn, &c. at the back of the inn; where are a rustic alcove, and two neat moss-houses.

This inn was formerly an obscure public-house, and owes much of its present celebrity to the conviviality of some of the first citizens of the metropolis. Their liberality has, however, been amply deserved by the excellent accommodations provided by the present proprietor and his family, who have possessed the concern from its first establishment. It has, during that time, been the favourite resort of the *bon-vivant;* and there are few to be met with, in the convivial circles of our metropolis, who have not passed many mirthful hours here; and many may well date the happiest period of their existence from this spot.*

Here the gallant Nelson, in company with Sir William and Lady Hamilton,

---

their boat, striking against it, was upset, and some of the party were drowned by the rapidity of the current.

* To my London acquaintance, I cannot suggest a pleasanter mode of passing a day, than by driving to this spot on a fine open morning, either in the months of May, enjoyed several days of calm retirement, a short time before he quitted England to take the command of that glorious expedition which raised him to immortality.

Hence the road crosses the Mole by *Burford-bridge*, and winds off to Dorking.

The following poetical description of these paradisiacal regions is from the pen of Mrs. Barbauld, on her experiencing their powerful attractions during a residence here for a few days.

What low building is that, so invitingly neat,
Where the way-faring man at the door finds a seat,
With prospects so enchanting his mind to refill?—
'Tis the cottage that stands at the foot of the hill.

From the smoke, and the din, and the hurry of town,
Let the care-wearied cit to this spot hasten down:
And, embosom'd in shades, hear the lark singing shrill
In the cottage that stands at the foot of the hill.

Let the fierce party-zealot suspend his alarms,
Nor here dream of invasion, or talk of arms;
Here the sweet charms of Nature his passions shall still,
As he treads the soft turf at the foot of the hill.

Here the belle, that is drooping from crowds and night-air,
May her freshness renew, and her roses repair;
And the sick gather health, without doctor or pill,
By a walk from the top to the foot of the hill.

Here's a health to the cottage, and health to the plains;
Ever blithe be your damsels, and constant your swains;
Here may Industry, Peace, and Contentment, reign still,
While the Mole softly creeps at the foot of the hill.

August, or September. On arriving at Box-Hill, I would recommend them to *breakfast;* after which, to follow the circuitous route described in the foregoing pages, and return to Box-Hill to *dinner*. This is a BILL OF FARE, which rivals with the luxurious excursions to the "LOVELIEST OF HILLS," whose resplendent beauties have been so sublimely commemorated by *the Poet of the year.*

My reader will readily imagine that I reluctantly take leave of such sublime subjects. Thousands have already revelled among the exquisite scenes which it has been my aim to describe, with a view of affording similar gratification to those who, hitherto, have not witnessed their beauties. The preceding pages consist of the recorded incidents of a single day; and those who *have* visited the respective sites have, I trust, retraced in this volume the most interesting features of their journey. The reflections deduced from them only serve to verify the old adage, viz. that " *art* is long, and *life* but short;" and it may be added, that the futility of the former, when compared with the lubricity of the latter, should teach us, like the Emperor VESPASIAN, to record the incidents of our lives; so that, on referring to the pages of our DIARY, we may there enjoy the unimpaired transports of a pleasing retrospect.

THE END.

J. and C. Adlard, Printers,
23, Bartholomew Close.